TRANSACTIONS

OF THE

AMERICAN PHILOSOPHICAL SOCIETY

HELD AT PHILADELPHIA
FOR PROMOTING USEFUL KNOWLEDGE

NEW SERIES—VOLUME 63, PART 1
1973

TEPEXI EL VIEJO:
A POSTCLASSIC FORTIFIED SITE IN THE MIXTECA-PUEBLA REGION OF MEXICO

SHIRLEY GORENSTEIN

Assistant Professor of Anthropology, Columbia University

THE AMERICAN PHILOSOPHICAL SOCIETY
INDEPENDENCE SQUARE
PHILADELPHIA

February, 1973

Library of Congress Catalog
Card Number 73–75472
International Standard Book Number 0–87169–631–2

PREFACE

National Science Foundation Grant No. GS-744 was given to support a specialized investigation of Tepexi el Viejo, Puebla, Mexico for the period May, 1965, until October, 1966. The summer of 1965 and part of the summer of 1966 was devoted to field work, and the remaining months were spent in laboratory analysis.

A permit to do the field work in Mexico was granted by the Instituto Nacional de Antropología e Historia, and the facilities of the Instituto Poblano de Antropología e Historia were provided for study and analysis. In this connection I wish to thank José Luis Lorenzo and Ephraim Castro. I am grateful to Ignacio Bernal for his interest and suggestions and to Roman Piña Chan for permission to examine the collection in the Museo Nacional de Antropología and to Donald Collier for permission to examine the Field Museum of Natural History collection.

I am also indebted to Harold E. Malde, Rhodes Fairbridge, Carl Fries, Maria Elena Landa Abrego, José Luis Franco, John Paddock, Barbro Dahlgren, Bruce Schroeder, Glen H. Cole, and Edward P. Lanning for professional help and guidance, and to Patricia Jane Feltham and Mark Druss who were field assistants during the 1965 season, and to Jonathan Horwitz for laboratory work.

I wish to thank Caroll Boltin not only for her illustrations, but also for her direction in presenting data graphically, Lee Boltin for photographing the artifacts, and Samuel Gorenstein for statistical aid.

I am most deeply indebted to Gordon Ekholm for his continuing guidance and for his permission to use the facilities of the American Museum of Natural History and to Robert Stigler who was a source of aid throughout the investigation.

This study is dedicated to Madeline Jo and Charles Michael in memory of their mother.

S. G.

TEPEXI EL VIEJO: A POSTCLASSIC FORTIFIED SITE IN THE MIXTECA–PUEBLA REGION OF MEXICO

Shirley Gorenstein

CONTENTS

INTRODUCTION

There have been two important foci for the study of early civilization: its emergence and the traits which define it. Mesoamericanists have been in the forefront of this investigation because of the considerable extant and potential data on this subject in that area. The evolution from simple to complex society has been studied in terms of the progression of society from one level of socio-cultural integration or stage to the next with the view that when society reaches the level or stage of "civilization" its characteristics can be described in general terms. There has been some consensus that any definition of civilization involves social, economic, political as well as technological criteria. Thus, although monumental architecture is listed, the emphasis is on other traits. The important social and economic traits are a large, dense population stratified on the basis of occupational specialization and differential access to strategic resources. The political aspect of civilization is the state which is defined by two primary traits. The first is the concentration of political power in a complex of institutions established on a non-kin basis, and the second is the use of force to maintain that power. These military-political traits are considered critical in the definition of civilization.

A theoretical framework for the investigation of the dynamics of cultural change not only from simple to complex society, but also from one sort of complex society to another is one which focuses on the variability of traits. If culture is considered a systemic whole, then the process of change may be seen through the analysis of a series of continuous system states (the state of a system involves a description of the current condition of the system adequate enough to predict future states of the system, and it is assumed that the relationships among the components of the system are known) in which components are not simply absent or present, but have different values from one system state to the next. Thus, determining the different values of traits is a means of determining change. An examination of the association of traits with different values may reveal dependent and independent variables, and, thus, provide the basis for recognizing the direction of change. No quantitative values need be assigned; rather qualitative differences can be noted. This method has been suggested by Mihajlo D. Mesarović (1968) in the investigation of biological systems.

The investigation of Tepexi el Viejo is part of a study of the military systems and their relationship to political systems in prehispanic Mesoamerica. The purpose of that study is to determine the processes by which the military-political systems of complex societies change in order, ultimately, to offer an explanatory statement concerning the direction of change.

Prehistoric military systems in the New World were highly varied, but this multiformity has been very little appreciated. Sites described as fortified are usually those which were *highly* fortified. Others, with unimpressive fortifications, are often classfied as without fortification.

From the archaeologist's point of view a military system consists of artifacts and features connected with warfare and the behavior of personnel related to them. Fortification is a general term defined as architecture and features, singly or in groups, that function in offensive and defensive action. Brush thrown across a road to hinder passage is a fortification, as is a specialized building set at a strategic point and used exclusively for military action. In this study terms such as "fortress" will not be imposed on a fortification without further definition. These are "portmanteaux" designations, carrying far more qualities than are usually appropriate to the architecture and features so labeled, and, in this way, obscuring their true function. An analytical approach will be used here in order to delineate precisely the exact nature of a fortification and its function.

Communities which engaged in warfare have been described indiscriminately as militaristic. Militarism, however, is properly defined as a preoccupation and intense concern with warfare. There were many military systems which functioned without this ethos. A society without militarism need not be without a military system, and a society with militarism may have a rudimentary military technology. It has been customary also to oppose the term theocratic to militaristic. There is, however, no reason to believe *a priori* that theocracies were not militaristic or even without warfare. There is nothing functionally incompatible between rule by priests and a militaristic system.

This study is based on the assumption that a variety of military systems existed in Postclassic Mexico, and it seeks to contribute to the understanding of this multiformity. The range of military systems can be, perhaps, circumscribed by what can be called specialized and non-specialized types. In a specialized system artifacts, structures, and personnel are all marked exclusively for warfare. A construction built for the purpose of guarding the entrance to a valley is a specialized fortification. A professional standing army whose members support themselves entirely by their preparation for and activity in war is a specialized force. In a non-specialized system artifacts, structures, and personnel serve several purposes simultaneously. For example, a wall which prevents erosion and also acts as a protective device for a settlement, or a militia called up only in time of crisis is non-specialized.

It is assumed that the varieties of military systems will be linked to a multiplicity of political systems, and that the relationship between the two systems will be dependent. Certain types of military systems support particular kinds of political systems which, in turn, are sustained by them. Political centralization refers to the relationship of one political system with others. In a fully centralized relationship political power resides in one system and is not shared with others with which it has ties. In other words, this kind of political system is characterized by the exclusive right to political power among articulating political systems. The other systems may have political functions, but do not have the right to make decisions. A completely decentralized relationship is one in which political power is apportioned out equally among related systems. A political state has some degree of political centralization.

It is the contention of this study that specialization in the military system and centralization of power in the political system are related variables. The greater the military specialization, the greater the political centralization, and conversely, the greater the military non-specialization, the greater the political decentralization.

All military systems contain both specialized and non-specialized components, and there are many degrees of centralization of political power. These complexities should not be overlooked for the purposes of generalization. They provide the varieties from which fitting, and therefore useful, generalizations may be deduced. But, more important, they show the processes of change. In the Aztec military organization, for example, professional soldiers existed along with noble warriors who had primarily social roles in warfare. The juxtaposition of both groups indicates flux. The chronological priority of the noble warriors suggests the change was from non-specialization to specialization in personnel, and this is in harmony with indications of attempts at greater political centralization at the same time.

My investigation of military systems began in 1961 when I undertook a comparison of Peruvian and Mesoamerican fortifications (Gorenstein, 1963, 1966*a*) It indicated that Peruvian fortifications were more specialized than Mesoamerican and political centralization was greater in the former area than in the latter. That study blocked out the critical variables, but did not show the varying relationships among them. The archaeological data on fortifications were not sufficient to permit discrimination among military parameters and their variable expressions.

In 1964 I sought a fortified site in Mesoamerica where I could investigate the interrelationships among the components of a military and political system. The area I chose to survey was central Mexico where several fortified sites existed in the Postclassic, that is, from about A.D. 900 to the Conquest in A.D. 1519 (Gorenstein, 1966*b*). After examining Huexotla, Cacaxtla, Itzocan, Huaquechula, and Tepexi el Viejo, I decided to work at the latter site because its military artifacts and features were unquestionable and in the best state of preservation.

Tepexi el Viejo is the Mixteca-Puebla region and is known from documentary evidence to have flourished in the Aztec period and to have been conquered by Cortés in 1520. Since the investigation focused on the military and political systems, field work was oriented towards this end. Emphasis was placed on mapping the site and obtaining a plan of the structural remains to determine the settlement and fortification pattern. Test pits were dug to clarify the nature of the structural remains and to obtain artifacts in a stratified sequence. The analysis of the ceramics yielded a chronological sequence and revealed Tepexi's relationship with other centers in Mesoamerica. The lithic analysis provided information on weapons used in warfare.

In addition to the archaeological data, historical sources have been searched and presented. The documentary evidence on Tepexi is considered an important complement to the archaeological. All the data have been examined within the context of the Mixteca-Puebla region as it is known archaeologically and historically.

In conclusion, the cultural history of Tepexi is presented, the military-political system of Tepexi, as an indication of the military-political system of Mixteca-Puebla communities, is discussed, and a conception of the process of change of military-political systems is offered.

ENVIRONMENT

Tepexi el Viejo is at a latitude of 18°35'04"W, a longitude of 97°59'46"N, and an altitude of 1,700 meters above sea level. It lies in the state of Puebla some fifty kilometers to the south and slightly to the east of the city of Puebla, and about six kilometers and 290° true bearing from the town of Tepexi de Rodríguez.

The southern Puebla area is related to the Balsas Depression in terms of physiography. The Depression lies between the Mexican Plateau and the highlands of Oaxaca and Guerrero. The Tepexi locality is characterized by low hills, formerly continuous surfaces, which are now deeply dissected by steep-walled valleys (Tamayo, 1949: pp. 417–418; West, 1964: pp. 60–62). The main area of the site occupies the northern end of one of these low hills. It is just south of the Xamilpan River, a permanent stream that flows into the Atoyac Poblano River which is a tributary of the Balsas River system that empties into the Pacific Ocean (Tamayo, 1946: pp. 276–297, map). The Xamilpan River is fed by a number of intermittent streams, and the water level is affected by the regime of long dry and short rainy periods (Comisión, 1958). The altitude of the Xamilpan River Valley is 1,539 meters.

Tepexi is in the *Tierra Templada* climatic zone. It has an average temperature of between 14° and 20° centigrade. It is difficult to distinguish seasons. December and January are the coldest months with an average of 14° centigrade, and April, May, June, and July are the months with the highest average temperature ranging from 18° to 20° centigrade. Since May, June, and July have considerable rainfall, the hottest month is April rather than the high-sun period of June and July. The months of heavy rain are May, June, August, September, and part of October when between 90 and 95 per cent of the yearly rainfall occurs. The total annual precipitation averages 800 mm. to 1,000 mm. (Vivó, 1964; Vivó and Gómez, 1946; Tamayo, 1946: Carta-Isoyetas; Carreño, 1951: Carta-Isoyetas).

The region is subject to thunderstorms which occur on the average of fifty days a year (Vivó and Gómez, 1946). There may have been greater thunderstorm activity in the past than at present at Tepexi since the site shows an apparent absence of erosion scars denuded of trees. In any case, as a result of intense rainfall, the valley walls at Tepexi are dissected by numerous gullies which produce a pronounced pattern of dendritic drainage (Malde, 1966: personal communication).

The soil is gray (10 YR 6/2, dry) for the most part, but there are places where it is red (5 YR 6/4, dry). An explanation for red beds has been given by Theodore Walker (1967: p. 353).

New evidence supports the theory that the hematite pigment in many red beds, particularly those associated with evaporites and aeolian sandstones, formed after deposition in hot arid or semi-arid climates. . . . The sequence in the Sonoran desert contains examples of red beds forming today in a hot dry climate. They are associated with bedded evaporites and occur where regional faunal, floral, and pedological evidence indicates rainfall has been low throughout the postdepositional history of the sediments. . . . these red-stained facies show progressive stages of *in situ* alteration of nonred sediments to hematite-stained red beds, and in each, the iron in the stain is derived from interstratal alteration of iron bearing detrital grains. . . .

Within less than 30 cm. of the surface an indurated laminar horizon of nearly pure carbonate is found. The carbonate horizon refers to a lime accumulation of a type known as caliche (and called locally *tepetate*). There has been difficulty in arriving at a definition of caliche because of its various forms, but, recently, an encompassing one was offered by Gile and others (1965: pp. 74, 82).

Accumulations of authigenic [generated on the spot, a term applied to minerals which originated in sediments at the time of or after deposition] carbonate [$CaCO_3$ and $MgCO_3$ are equivalent in per cent with $CaCO_3$ dominant] are common in soils of arid regions and in many of these soils form prominent layers in which morphology is determined by the impregnating carbonate; such layers can be considered soil horizons . . . [because] they parallel the soil surface; their upper boundaries commonly occur within several inches to about two feet of the soil surface; they have distinctive morphologies of overlying and underlying horizons containing relatively little carbonate; they occur in sediments of various compositions and textures; and they form in a developmental sequence. . . . Though these horizons display a variety of macroscopic forms and range in consistency from soft to extremely hard, they all have a peculiar and diagnostic soil fabric, the K-fabric . . . fine grained authigenic carbonate coats or engulfs skeletal pebbles, sand and silt grains as an essentially continuous medium.

In discussing formation of the K horizon Gile and others (1966: p. 384) have written:

Some parent sediments are noncalcareous, whereas others are derived primarily from limestone. However, analyses of dust fall for four seasons indicate that calcareous dust has been deposited on all sediments. On each wetting a small portion of the carbonate in the dust would be dissolved, moved into the soil and there precipitated as the water evaporates. Thus, regardless of composition of the sediment, all soils are considered to have a calcareous parent material. A calcareous dust source for carbonate provides an explanation for the occurrence of equally prominent carbonate horizons in calcareous and noncalcareous sediments of the same age. . . . The carbonate morphological sequences [which are presented in this article] . . . suggest strongly that the authigenic carbonate is illuvial. The ubiquity of calcareous dust suggests that authigenic carbonate was derived dominantly to wholly, or in calcareous sediments, in part from the dust fall.

K horizons of varying morphologies are found throughout Mexico. The caliche at Tepexi is indurated and white (10 YR 9/2). For building purposes it is good and durable, similar to limestone.

Very little soil now remains on the hill or slopes of Tepexi. The caliche is exposed in many places, and, at present, little cultivation is possible. The present natural vegetation of the region can be classified on the broadest level as of the seasonal formation series. It is a tropical thorn scrub forest composed of tall columnar cactus (*Cephalocereus*) as well as many other cacti; izote or yucca (*Yucca*); low piny shrubs such as *Castela*; *Schaefferia*; *Gochnatis*; succulents such as *Euphorbia, Acanthothamnus, Pedilanthus*; and *Agave*; and associations of deciduous trees and shrubs. However, the region now suffers from the results of intensive erosion, and the original natural cover was probably different from what it is today (Miranda, 1947: pp. 95–96; Wagner, 1964: pp. 251–253).

The locality supports very few fauna. Iguanas, racerunner lizards, and cottontails have been reported. Certainly the natural vegetation can now sustain little else.

The documentary evidence makes it clear that there was considerable cultivation of a number of crops at Tepexi in prehispanic times. The first information comes from the reports concerning the tribute Tepexi and twenty-two other towns under Tepeaca were required to pay to the Mexicans after 1503.

According to Borah and Cook's (1963: p. 136) interpretation of the documents this group provided once a year 1 crib of maize, 1 crib of beans, 1 crib of lime-leaved sage, and 1 crib of *huautli*. In addition every eighty days they gave 8,000 loads of canes for arrows, 4,000 loads of lime, 200 carrying frames, 800 loads of rolled units of tobacco, and 800 deer hides. While other communities were taxed manufactured goods, such as mantles, gold disks, and turquoise masks, these were assessed products of the land. The Mexican appraisal of these towns' economy points to two things: the lack of manufacturing industries and an adequate, and perhaps abundant, production of cultivated plants and collected natural resources.

Similarly, a tribute record (see below) reflecting conditions during the same years indicates that Tepexi's tributaries were responsible for furnishing manufactured goods, while the population of Tepexi and its environs provided their lords with agricultural products and animals. While irrigation ditches have not been recovered archaeologically, this document clearly states that Tepexi had irrigated as well as non-irrigated lands. The irrigated lands were probably within the Tepexi locality itself. The products of the irrigated lands are recorded as cotton, maize, pumpkins, and hot peppers. The non-irrigated lands must have been a kilometer and more to the west where the low altitude and higher rainfall would have permitted the cultivation of the crops listed as grown on non-irrigated land such as cacao which could not grow at the Tepexi locality without irrigation.

Cultivation of this order must have been possible because the area had not yet suffered the worst effects of the progressive soil erosion which reached its height in postconquest times. The question of preconquest soil erosion has been discussed by Miranda (1947), Cook (1949), and more recently by Wagner (1964), Byers (1967a), and Flannery and others (1967). From these studies it seems clear that soil erosion was accelerated by prehispanic and posthispanic agriculture practices, and in certain areas it was more of a problem than in others before the conquest.

The geological and archaeological data leave no doubt that erosion was continuous throughout the occupation of the settlement. There was considerable gullying of hillslopes, and great walls functioned to prevent the diminution of the surface by erosion. This is especially evident on the eastern slope of the hill where a steep gully terminates at the wall (Malde, 1966: personal communication). But there was, apparently, enough land under cultivation to maintain the population. When Tepexi was taxed agricultural products by the Mexicans and later by the Spaniards, it appears that it was the greater demands on the ultimately limited land, not erosion, that precipitated a community crisis (Gorenstein, 1969).

The Xamilpan Valley and the hillslopes below the main precinct were cultivated. Low walls constructed on the hillslopes indicate the use of a *lama-bordo* system, that is, the water and eroding soils from the hilltop and higher hillslopes were trapped by dikes, and highly fertile terraced plots were created (*cf.* Spores, 1969: p. 563). The effects of erosion accelerated by agricultural practices and scattered artifacts as well as the remains of small structures indicate that the hilltop south of the main precinct and Subsite II and the hilltops immediately to the northeast and southwest were also cultivated.

The lands of Tepexi, however, apparently extended several kilometers from the settlement. As has been noted above, the Tepexi tribute record states that cacao was cultivated on non-irrigated land belonging to Tepexi itself. Since cacao cannot be grown at the Tepexi locality, but can a kilometer or more to the west, it seems that Tepexi's lands must have extended in this direction at least. Lands extending some distance from the main settlement is a Mixtec pattern known from historical sources (*cf.* Spores, 1967: pp. 93–94). These lands seem to have been attached to independent hamlets which were an integral part of the center community.

Tepexi el Viejo today is barren and deserted. The archaeological and ethnohistorical evidence indicates that it was a thriving center for more than two hundred years before the Conquest. The environmental information offers part of the explanation for its prosperity. The conditions of the land appear to have been different then from what they are today. At that time the land was highly cultivable, and the technology was adequate enough to decelerate the slow process of soil erosion. The result was a balanced relationship between the needs of the population and the capacity of the environment.

ARCHAEOLOGICAL BACKGROUND

Tepexi is in the archaeological region which in the Postclassic was dominated by the Mixteca-Puebla style. That style has been found at sites concentrated primarily in Puebla, the Mixteca, the Valley of Oaxaca, and parts of Tlaxcala and Veracruz. The term Mixteca-Puebla was devised by George Vaillant (1944: pp. 41, 42, 94) to deal with several elements at once: the tribal group known historically as the Mixtecs, the region occupied by the Nahua-speaking tribes in Puebla and the Mixtecs in northern Oaxaca, and a distinctive political history, religion, iconography, and art style. Vaillant used the term in various ways. He referred to a Mixteca-Puebla "period," culture," "civilization," and "culture complex."

The problem here is a perennial one in archaeology. The archaeologist is aware that the material aspects of a culture are accompanied by the non-material, and so readily, and even justifiably, uses holistic terms such as "culture" and "culture complex," even though little of the non-material culture is known. In the case at hand, the archaeologist has documentary evidence on the Mixtec people from protohistoric and early historic sources, but even with this, it has not been easy to link the prehistoric culture with its protohistoric and early historic descendant. We really do not know much about the Postclassic society and culture which produced the historic Mixtecs, and the Mixteca-Puebla influence throughout Mesoamerica has been identified primarily through stylistic elements. H. B. Nicholson (1960: p. 30) has described the elements of the Mixteca-Puebla style, some of which are distinctive, others are pan-Mesoamerican:

. . . [t]he style at its best . . . is characterized by an almost geometric precision in delineation. Symbols are standardized and rarely so highly conventionalized that their original models cannot be ascertained. Colors are numerous, vivid, and play an important symbolic role in themselves. . . . The presence [of certain distinctive] . . . symbols or a characteristic grouping is often enough in itself to define the presence of the style. [among them] are: solar and lunar disks, celestial and terrestial bands, the Venus bright star symbol, skulls and skeletons, . . . jade, . . . water, fire and flames, heart, war, . . . mountain or place, "downy feather ball," flower, stylized eyes as stars, stepped fret, . . . sliced spiral shell, . . . and twenty *tonalpohualli* signs. One of the most frequent and diagnostic symbol groups is the row of alternating skulls and crossed bones (often combined with hearts, severed hands, etc.). Zoomorphic forms are quite distinctive and easily recognizable, particularly serpents . . . jaguars, deer, rabbits, and spiders. The many deities depicted are highly individualized and usually accompanied by special, clearly distinguishable insignia.

The broad spatial distribution (to Tamuín in the Huasteca, Guasave, Sinaloa, Yucatan, British Honduras, Guatemala, Salvador, and, possibly, to Nicaragua and Costa Rica) and the stylistic complexity and distinctiveness suggest to Nicholson that the Mixteca-Puebla style might be seen best as a horizon style despite its temporal longevity. The single term, "Mixtec," for the style is not employed here for the reasons Nicholson (1961) has given so cogently: the Mixtec expression of the horizon style is a local manifestation, that is, it does not extend throughout the region in which the style predominates, and the term "Mixtec" alone implies occupation by Mixtec speakers, and other languages were important in the region. There are also indications that Puebla may be of greater importance than the Mixteca as a center of Mixtec culture. Dropping the term "Puebla" leads to an emphasis on the Mixteca at the expense of Puebla (map 1).

Although the origins of the Mixteca-Puebla style are not known precisely, the evidence we have at this time indicates that Cholula and southern Puebla were the critical areas in the initial development and continuing influence of the style which was expressed in the Mixteca and elsewhere as substyles. According to Noguera (1954, 1965), the earliest full manifestation of the style is perhaps at Cholula with the appearance of the so-called *policroma laca* and the *decoración negra sobre fondo natural del barro* of the Cholulteca I-Altar de Craneos period. The *policroma laca* was contemporaneous with the construction of the last pyramid and the important monuments at Cholula. The number and depth of the strata in which this pottery appears in abundant quantities indicate to Noguera that Cholulteca I was a long period. Nicholson (1961) suggests that in the late Classic, when both Teotihuacan and Monte Albán were declining, the Mixteca-Puebla style was developing somewhere to the east and south of the Valley of Mexico with Cholula, possibly, as the center. He suggests that Xochicalco, where sculpture motifs foreshadow the Mixteca-Puebla style, may have been a bridge between the older and newer styles. At the same time another style was developing north of Teotihuacan with Tula as the center. The two styles had considerable influence on each other. Their meeting in the southern Valley of Mexico can be seen at Chalco where the ceramics show strong Cholula influence. Apparently the southern style ultimately dominated the northern one since the Toltec seems to be a substyle of the Mixteca-Puebla despite its unique features.

According to Jiménez Moreno (1942, 1966), the dominance of Cholula and the emergence of the Mixteca-Puebla style *par excellence* there can be linked to the dynasty of the Olmeca-Xicalanca, known through ethnohistoric sources. He notes that the documentary sources indicate that the progenitors of the Mixtec dynasties of the codices, which record events dating back to earlier than A.D. 690 (Caso, 1949), originally

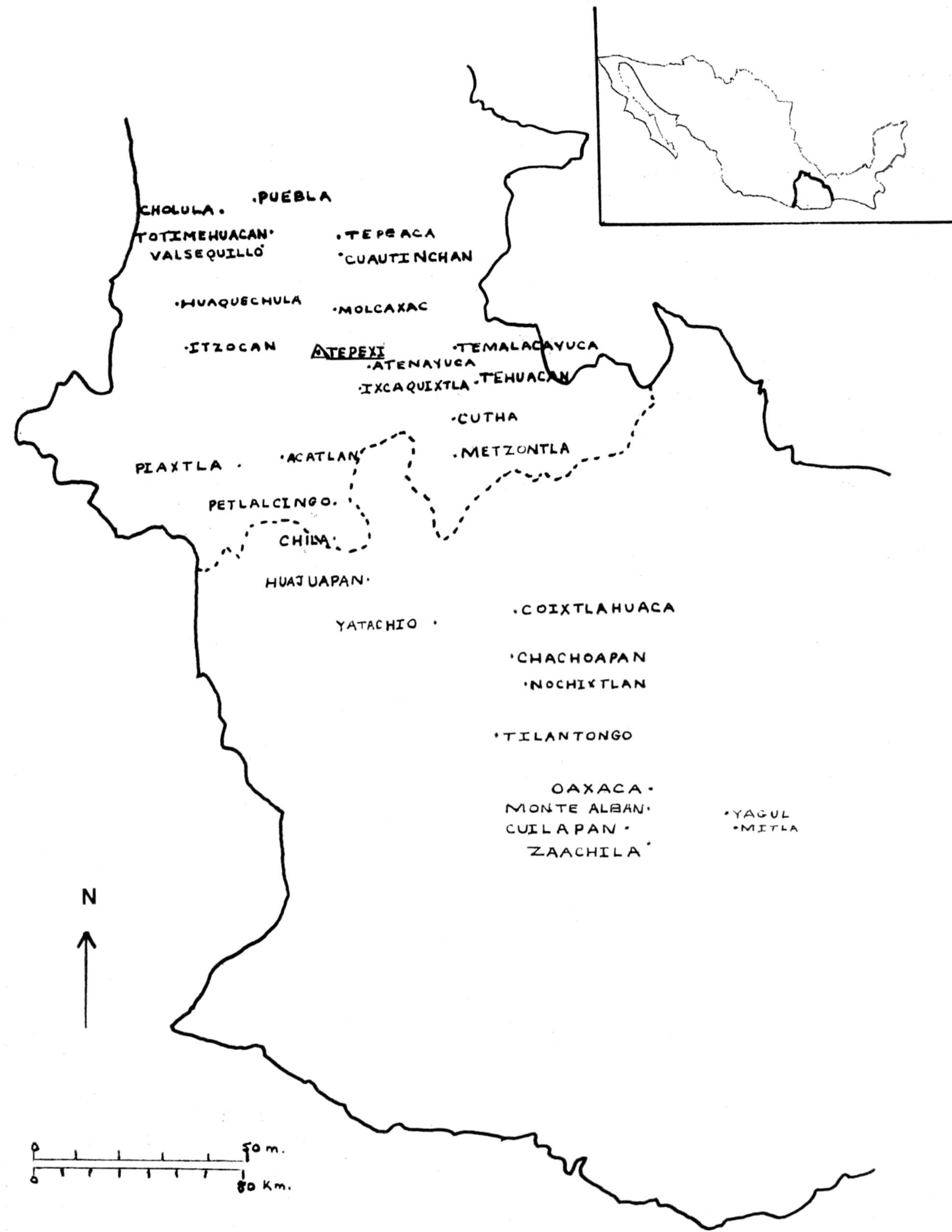

MAP 1. The Mixteca-Puebla region.

came from Teotitlan del Camino, established themselves in Apoala, and later founded the Tilantongo kingdom in A.D. 720. The people of Tilantongo became part of the Olmeca-Xicalanca who consisted of Nahua, Mixtec, and Chocho-Popoloca speakers and who conquered Cholula around A.D. 800, or perhaps earlier, displacing the Teotihuacan group in power and initiating the Mixteca-Puebla style. During their reign they seem to have had some control over territory in Puebla, Tlaxcala, the southern basin of Mexico, and the Valley of Morelos and would seem to have been contending with the political ambitions of the Toltecs. Their domination of Cholula ended after the fall of Tula when Toltec immigrants wrested power from the Olmeca-Xicalanca and drove them out of Cholula at a date variously calculated as A.D. 1168, A.D. 1240, and A.D. 1292.

It is especially important for this study to note that people who spoke Nahua, Mixtec and Chocho-Popoloca lived together in southern Puebla around Itzocan, Acatlan, and Tepexi in the sixteenth century. Jiménez Moreno (1966) has suggested that the Olmeca-Xicalanca originated in that part of the Mixteca-Puebla region. John Paddock (1966), in a connected hypothesis, has suggested that the Mixteca-Puebla style is an indigenous development from an earlier local style which he has called Ñuiñe dated A.D. 200 to A.D. 700 and placed in the region between the Cholula highlands and the Mixteca Alta.

The Toltecs apparently were able to fuse their own style, already shaped by the Mixteca-Puebla style, with the purer version at Cholula, so that the Cholulteca tradition appears to continue with very little change. Cholulteca II may be represented by *policroma mate* although the dating of this type is not firm. Cholulteca III was the last period before contact, and is represented by *policroma firme* (Noguera, 1965).

Ignacio Bernal (1965) in a recent synthesis has suggested that the Mixteca-Puebla style first arose in the Mixteca, not Cholula, in the tenth century and showed subsequent Toltec affinities. He bases his interpretation on what he sees as Coyotlatelco and Mazapan influences in Mixteca ceramics.

Evelyn Rattray (1966) has offered a different interpretation of Coyotlatelco pottery. Her study has led her to suggest that Coyotlatelco is not a component of the Toltec complex. Rather, she proposes, it was associated with the agricultural Otomí who, possibly, were driven from the Valley of Mexico at the time of the Toltec invasion. Coyotlatelco pottery is found at Cholula, and, subsequently, a Red/Cream ware appears in the Mixteca Alta. Perhaps Coyotlatelco pottery is the stylistic source for this ware.

In any case the two important regions for the evolving Mixteca-Puebla style in the Postclassic were Puebla and the Mixteca. It is difficult to delineate the boundaries of the Mixteca-Puebla style in Puebla. Too little work has been done and only individual sites can be identified. The major work has been done at Cholula (Noguera, 1954) and Tehuacan (Byers, 1967b). (All the volumes of the report on Tehuacan have not been released at the time of this writing.) Some excavations and observations have been made at Calipan, Tepeaca, and Cuthá (Noguera, 1940, 1945, 1954, 1960; Cassío, 1940), and the pottery from Acatlan has been accorded some study (Seler-Sachs, 1949; Franco, 1955; Foster, 1960). As part of this investigation surface collections were taken from Itzocan, Huaquechula, Molcaxac and Tepeaca, and surface collections at the Instituto Poblano de Antropología e Historia from Chiquihuite (near Totimehuacan), San Francisco de Asis Tetela (in the vicinity of Valsequillo), Tepozuchil (just east of the city of Puebla), and Acatlan were examined.

The Mixteca lies approximately between the latitudes of 16° and 18°15′W and the longitudes of 97° and 98°30′N, covering an area of some 40,000 kilometers. The western border is approximately the same as the western border of the present state of Oaxaca, but occasionally encroaches upon the present state of Guerrero. The northern border includes some of southern Puebla (but not Tepexi). Its limits are Tuzantlán on the west and Cañada on the east. The eastern border begins at Cañada and follows the valleys in Oaxaca until the town of Cuilapan where it turns towards the south-southwest following the mountains to the town of Teojomulco where it turns south-southeast passing through the region around the town of Cuixtla and finally turns south reaching the coast near Puerto Angel. The southern boundary is the Pacific Ocean. The Mixteca is divided into three major physiographic regions: the Mixteca Alta which is in the east-central part of the Mixteca, the Mixteca Baja in the north and west, and the Mixteca de la Costa in the south (Dahlgren, 1954: pp. 15–17) (map 2).

Very little work has been done in the Mixteca Baja and the Mixteca de la Costa. In the Mixteca Alta, Coixtlahuaca, Chachoapan, Tilantongo, Yatachío, and the Nochistlan Valley are the only sites where any systematic investigation has been undertaken (Bernal, 1948–1949, 1953; Caso, 1938, 1942; Spores, 1969).

The Mixteca-Puebla style seems to have moved from the Mixteca Alta eastward to the Valley of Oaxaca. There is a certain florescence of style in the Valley of Oaxaca, perhaps because of the stimulation by the earlier Zapotec culture, which was still viable in the Valley after the advent of the Mixtecs. The only sites in the Valley that have been investigated to any extent are Mitla, Yagul, Monte Albán, Cuilapan, and Zaachila (Caso and Rubín de la Borbolla, 1936; Paddock, 1960; Caso, 1932; Bernal, 1958, 1966a; Gallegos, 1962; Wicke, 1966). However, the Valley as a whole has been under study in recent years (Flannery and others, 1967). Bernal (1966a: pp. 363–365) has suggested that there were two different "Mixtec-influenced"

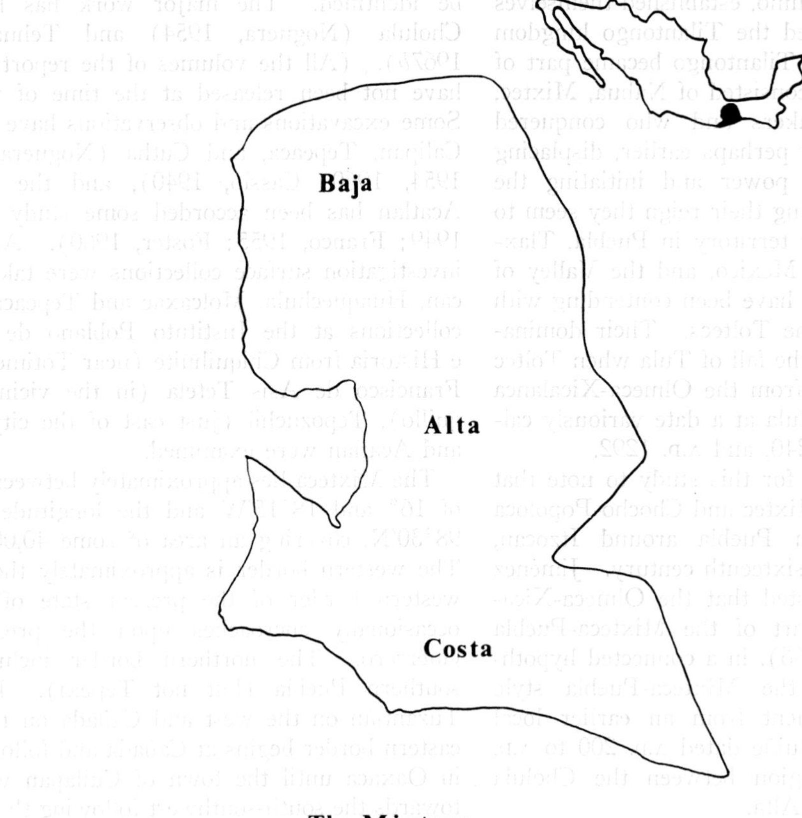

MAP 2. The Mixteca.

groups in the Valley: an eastern group found at Mitla and Yagul, and a western group at Monte Albán, Cuilapan, and Zaachila. The Mixteca-Puebla style as it is manifested in the western group is similiar to that found in the Mixteca Alta. But the eastern group, although it shares some traits with the western and the Mixteca Alta, has its own character.

Analyses of the ceramics from the Mixteca-Puebla region are not numerous. Types found at individual sites in the Valley of Oaxaca are known, but there are too few data at this time to characterize these regions as wholes. There has been some success in delineating the characteristic types for Cholula and the Mixteca Alta.

According to Noguera (1954: pp. 85–142, 1965: pp. 104–109) there are four groups of decorated pottery which characterize the Mixteca-Puebla style at Cholula: *decoración sencilla, decoración roja o negra sobre fondo anaranjado, decoración negra sobre fondo color natural del barro,* and *cerámica policroma.*

The paste of the *decoración sencilla* is generally of a reddish-brown, not always of fine texture, but well-fired. A common form is the bowl with slightly convex high walls and a flat conical base. An orange paint applied to the interior of vessels is uneven, and the brush strokes are visible. There is a wide interior border with geometric motifs in dark red. The *decoración roja o negra sobre fondo anaranjado* has a fine-textured reddish paste, and is well-fired. The most common form is a flat plate without supports or with cylindrical or crenellated supports. Both the exterior and most of the interior surfaces are covered with an orange slip, and the decorative motifs are in black or red. *Decoración negra sobre fondo color natural del barro,* related to Culhuacan Black/Orange, is of a fine-textured paste and is well-fired. The bowl and plate are common forms both with and without supports. Geometric motifs are used, and, in addition, there are naturalistic and symbolic motifs.

Noguera has divided the *cerámica policroma* into *policroma laca, policroma mate,* and *policroma firme,* claiming that they have discrete chronological distribution. *Policroma laca* corresponds to Cholulteca I and is characterized by the fugitive quality of the paint. It yields easily to pressure and flakes so readily that there are few examples left with the decoration intact. Forms include the plate with zoomorphic supports, the goblet with circular supports, the incense burner with horzontal handle and vertical zoomorphic handle and with a handle with circular perforations, the bowl with concave base and small circular supports, the jar with wide spout and vertical handle, and a large cylindrical vase with circular supports. *Policroma mate* is distiguished by its matt surface and is tentatively assigned to Cholulteca II. The bowl and plate with small conical supports are the distinctive forms. *Policroma firme* corresponds to Cholulteca III and is characterized by the luster and firmness of its paint and by the attention paid to the decoration of borders. The plate is the most frequent form. Geometric as well as naturalistic and stylized motifs are used in *policroma laca* and the *policroma firme,* but only geometric motifs are found in the *policroma mate.* Many colors were used, but white, orange, black, and red predominate.

A variety of supports appear in the collection from Cholula. Noguera distinguishes conical, cylindrical, extended, flat, and crenelated supports, as well as zoomorphic and anthropomorphic. Spindle whorls are common. They are discoidal or conical with incised and stamped decorations.

The predominant pottery for the Mixteca Alta is a polished, well-fired, fine gray ware which is sometimes slipped in black with a painted band around the neck. Tripod bowls of this ware at times have a stamped base and elongated zoomorphic supports. Other common forms are globular tripod jars with cylindrical necks, pitchers with vertical necks and handles, and goblets with pedestal supports. Another ware found in the Mixteca Alta is of light reddish-brown clay with a variety of forms, although the large jar with a high neck and small handles on its globular body is most frequent. The two-legged perforated incense burner with a long handle made of fine brown-red clay is characteristic of the region.

Decorated wares are red on polished cream with geometric, anthropomorphic, and zoomorphic motifs; a black (graphite) on polished red with geometric motifs; and an unpolished red on cream. The most famous decorated ware of the Mixteca Alta is the polychrome. There is no question that it is related to the polychrome ware at Cholula. There is a vast variety of forms. The colors, predominantly black, white, yellow, pink, red, and orange, were painted over a brown ground and the surface was polished to a luster. Motifs are geometric, naturalistic, and symbolic. They are similar to those of the Mixtec codices (Caso and Bernal, 1965: pp. 892–895; Noguera, 1965: pp. 117–119).

The stonework and the work in copper and gold of the Mixtecs are known from public and private collections, but not so well known from archaeological investigations. The principal exception is Caso's discovery of Tomb 7 at Monte Albán. Fine work was done in jade, obsidian, turquoise, and rock crystal, as well as shell, coral, and pearl. Many fine pieces were made of gold, silver, and copper. Tin and lead seem to

have been used also. Although most of the metal objects are decorative pieces, Caso has pointed out that many utilitarian objects were made of metal also (Caso, 1965).

It is not possible as yet to describe the architectural style of the Mixteca-Puebla region because few ruins have been investigated. Most of what we know comes from illustrations in the Mixtec codices. Temples, palaces, adoratorios, ball courts, and sweat baths were all built. Tombs were cut into the caliche. Façades were elaborately sculptured and painted, as was common throughout Mesoamerica. Flat roofs with crenelations, mound platforms, stairways, and balustrades were all used. The houses of farmers were probably made of wattle and daub and adobe with thatch roofs.

HISTORICAL BACKGROUND

The understanding of the Postclassic culture of the Mixteca-Puebla region is aided considerably by historical information. There is a group of preconquest pictorial documents that have been identified as Mixtec. Those concerned primarily with the genealogies of the ruling families, political and military events, are the Codices Vienna, Nuttall, Selden, and Bodley. The Codices Borgia, Laud, Fejérváry-Mayer, Cospi, Vaticanus B, and the Mexican Manuscript No. 20 of the Bibliothèque Nationale in Paris are primarily concerned with mythology and religion (Robertson, 1966). In addition, there are the sixteenth-century Spanish chronicles and many kinds of administrative documents. The identity of the historic Mixtecs of the Spanish accounts with the Mixtecs of the codices, and these both with the inhabitants of the Mixteca-Puebla region known only archaeologically is somewhat tenuous. Nevertheless, these prehispanic and posthispanic documents offer invaluable data that are not now, and, in some cases, never will be, brought forth archaeologically.

Only historical data have been used in the following interpretive synthesis (based on Icaza, 1928; Paso y Troncoso, 1906; Herrera, 1947; Burgoa, 1934; Caso, 1949, 1960a, 1962, 1964, 1966; Dahlgren, 1954; Spores, 1967) of military-political organization in the Mixteca-Puebla region in the Postclassic. The description is probably most valid for the sixteenth century and weakest for the early Postclassic. It is, therefore, difficult to suggest the processes of institutional change that took place in that period of seven or eight hundred years.

The major centers in the Mixteca were Tilantongo, Coixtlahuaca, Tlaxiaco, Yanhuitlán, and Tututepec. They each held substantial tributary territory. Tututepec, in the Mixteca de la Costa, seems to have possessed the most extensive and stable realm. However, there is no indication that it or any of the other centers were dominant over the rest, and it would not be correct to speak of a politically unified Mixtec empire with a single capital. Nor were the political ties between a center and its territorial tributaries very strong. Tributaries were almost entirely autonomous. While the main political official was appointed by the ruler of the center, the appointee was a member of the tributary community, or, if he was not, he was connected to it by marriage. The center sent no colonists, governors, or garrison troops to the tributaries to establish primary political control over them. Tributaries were not absorbed by the center, but were circumjacent to it.

The rulers of these centers were in a carefully calculated line of succession. Genealogies, according to the codices and early Spanish documents, were kept with fine attention. Direct lineal descent and legitimacy were critical in inheritance. Illegitimate offspring could not inherit. All legitimate children were provided for (daughters as well as sons, although there was male preference) by inheriting from both mother and father. Inheritance from the father was primary, however. All those of the royal line were entitled to *cacicazgos,* and it is estimated that the majority received their due.

If parental resources were insufficient to satisfy the members of the line, warfare provided a solution. The ruler of a center who had defeated another would arrange for a member of his own line to rule. In this way, a domain was created for the royal person. Most important, the vanquished center was then connected to the first by a familial tie.

Marriage was probably the more common device used to obtain a domain. If two centers were not connected by blood, they were in a state of belligerency. A political marriage secured cooperative relations between them. In this way, one heir secured his birthright, and another, who had already received his domain, bought some measure of security for it.

The ruling families of the Mixteca, descended as they were from one dynasty, shared a cultural heritage. Contact among the members of the noble class seems to have been frequent, and provided the opportunity for a continuing social and cultural interchange. As a result, those aspects of life which were their particular province, such as government, the operation of the military, certain religious ceremonies, and the style of luxury goods were similar. The so-called "nationalist sentiment" and cultural coherence among the Mixtecs can be credited to this kin network that fostered and facilitated communication among a small group of governing nobles.

Very little is known about Mixtec social structure. There is no question, however, that there was class stratification. The noble class was a hereditary aristocracy whose status was traditionally ascribed. It strengthened and perpetuated its status by its control over economic resources. This class had exclusive political power. However, since it was not possible for every noble to receive a *cacicazgo,* there was dif-

ferential political power among members of the class. Some nobles were in primary positions as rulers, the others served in secondary places, for example, as administrators. While there may also have been differential economic control, both groups, unlike any other class were entitled to tribute.

The commoners consisted of traders, artisans, and farmers. It seems that traders could achieve considerable wealth. Tenant farmers and slaves were set apart as the lowest social group.

Both nobles and commoners fought in war. There is no indication of a society of warriors or of soldiering as an occupational specialty. Unlike the Aztecs, Mixtec commoners do not seem to have been able to achieve wealth and position through military success. The army mirrored the social structure. The *barrio* constituted the basic fighting unit, and *barrio* chiefs were leaders of the contingent in war.

Mixtec history is marked by warfare. There were, of course, the wars with the Zapotecs and Mexicans in which the Mixtecs attempted to preserve their economic as well as political independence. But the military reputation of Mixtecs is really based on the interminable internal wars that racked the region. There were the wars of the larger kingdoms in places far from the center, and there were the battles and skirmishes between communities of varying sizes. Most wars were for the purpose of increasing the number of tributary towns and villages. This was done by invading previously unsubjected lands and by fighting other Mixtec kingdoms for the prize of tributaries.

Since the minor centers had insufficient resources to support the military force necessary for forays into distant lands to conquer virgin towns, they were limited to wrangling for the tributary towns and villages already pledged to other Mixtec centers. In wars between centers, the tributaries were shifted from the register of the defeated center to that of the victor. The tributaries themselves were not invaded. They were merely the spoils of war.

While war was the result of competition among centers, it was also a source of cooperation. Centers which were allied by kinship were bound to come to each other's support. In addition, tributaries were sometimes taxed military aid. In wartime a center would call upon a tributary for men and supplies.

Some wars seem to be related to the institution of royal succession. The member of a royal line, who was not otherwise provided for, obtained a *cacicazgo* through military victory, as we have seen. When succession after the death of a ruler was not clear, the interregnum was apparently a time of warfare when contending lineages from different centers fought for the right to appoint the next *cacique.*

What does not seem to have been at issue were new lands for occupation. Nor did the need for sacrificial victims launch wars. This ritual was not so intensively practiced by the Mixtecs as by the Mexicans (possibly because of differential population pressure), and the acquisition of victims was probably a by-product of war, not in itself either a cause or goal in fighting.

The military system of the Postclassic in this region is exemplified by fortifications, a range of weapons, and militarism.

Communities or portions of communities were placed on hilltops which were more easily defended than valley sites. In addition, lookout posts, ditches, and walls were used to complement the natural advantage of the hilltop. The use of fortified hills both for defense and for regrouping preceding a surprise attack seems to have been widespread among the Mixtecs. Yanhuitlán, Sosola, and Coixtlahuaca are cited as having employed such installations, but there is very little other information in the historical sources on fortifications.

Weapons fall into the classes of missile, hand-to-hand and defense. The missile weapons were the bow and arrow, the dart and atlatl, and the sling. The bow and arrow are seen rarely in the codices (Codex Borgia: sheet 25; Codex Vaticanus B: sheets 31, 62 are possible illustrations). An exception, apparently, is the Codex Bodley where they are shown frequently (Dahlgren, 1954: p. 195). Darts are shown with the atlatl, but most frequently alone (Codex Borgia: sheets 2, 4, 6, 7, 8, 9, 16, 19, 22, 23, 42, 48, 62, 64, 65, 71; Codex Vaticanus B: sheets 6, 7, 25, 57, 70, 80, 81, 82, 83, 84; Codex Fejérváry-Mayer: sheets 2, 3). While the sling is known to have existed, it does not seem to be represented in the codices or perhaps it is too difficult to recognize because of its lack of distinct form.

The lance, a thrusting or stabbing weapon used in hand-to-hand combat, is mentioned in historical accounts, but it is hard to identify in the codices because size is not always represented proportionally. Without this datum it is not easy to differentiate between lances and darts (possible depictions are Codex Borgia: sheets 23, 25, 50, 53, 54; Codex Fejérváry-Mayer: sheet 37; Codex Vaticanus B: sheets 22, 28, 87, 92). There were two kinds: one with a point and the other with a point and blades inserted along the sides of the shaft near the point.

Another hand-to-hand weapon was the sword. There were four types, all sharing the characteristic feature of a wooden shaft with inserted blades. The first type had no point and the shaft was set in a handle. The second type was the same except it was much longer. The third type was the same as the first, but had a point, and the fourth was a single curved piece of wood with blades running from the end to the bottom of the curve, usually on the outer edge (Codex Vaticanus B: sheets 33, 52).

The third hand-to-hand weapon may have been the axe which had a head of stone or copper set into a handle of wood. Its short head and wide blade were designed for cutting. The rear of the head was fitted tightly into the handle so that it would not be dislodged when swung or after a blow was struck. It is depicted both in association with the glyph for war and also as a wood-cutting tool. Axes in a war context are in the Codex Borgia (sheets 19, 47, 52). In the Codex Fejérváry-Mayer (sheets 28, 38) the axe is shown as a wood-cutting tool.

The defensive weapons were the shield, armor, and the helmet. The shield was carried by means of straps that fitted over the left wrist and hand. They were made of cane, fiber, and wood, and were small (body protection was sacrificed for mobility) and round. A shield with darts behind it formed the glyph for war (*yaoyotl*) and is frequently found in the Borgia Group codices (Codex Borgia: sheets 5, 8, 13, 15, 17, 25, 27, 42, 43, 45, 47, 49, 52, 54, 55, 59, 63, 70, 75, 76; Codex Vaticanus B: sheets 7, 19, 30, 50, 51, 52, 59, 86; Codex Fejérváry-Mayer: sheets 18, 44).

Armor was of two kinds. The first was a short buckler of padded cotton, and the second was the skin of an animal worn over most of the body. Padded armor was a good defense against projectile points as well as the thrusting or stabbing lance and the striking sword. The animal skin was sufficient to deflect the tiny poisoned arrows.

Only ceremonial helmets are illustrated in the codices (Codex Fejérváry-Mayer: sheets 27, 32), but there is mention of helmets in historical sources, and it is likely there were more utilitarian types than those we see drawn in the pictorial documents.

There is very little evidence of tactics or strategy in the codices or historical accounts. It is said that captains (who were *barrio* chiefs or priests) fought only with captains and ordinary warriors with each other. Since the captains appear to have been an elite shock troop, this division seems to have been a military tactic as well as a response to the social structure. The range of weapons suggests that a series of tactical maneuvers may have been used.

Militarism, the intense concern with war and its apparatus, seems to have been part of the Mixtec military system. The drawings of warriors show them in splendid regalia, and weapons are depicted frequently in the codices. Because warriors and weapons are elaborated upon in these documents, it seems likely that warfare was a matter of especial interest. Militarism supports the development of military technology. If honor follows military success, then it is worth working to improve strategy, tactics, and weaponry in order to achieve victory and then glory. The display of war motifs in the codices is not only evidence of the existence of a military system, but also of the ethos which was part of that system.

The historical information permits us to draw a picture with a few clear although gross images. The rulers of the communities of the Mixteca-Puebla region, because of war, and in spite of continuing skirmishes, achieved political domination over tributary territories. The centers demanded tribute from the tributaries, but permitted them their political autonomy. And while the device of family ties linked centers, it did not provide a focus. The result was that political power was diffused within the Mixteca-Puebla as a whole and even within local territorial domains.

HISTORY OF TEPEXI FROM DOCU-MENTARY SOURCES

The documentary informaton on Tepexi is very thin. The greatest lack is the loss of its *Relación*. Paso y Troncoso wrote in 1906 that it was lost or in private hands. He had sought it without success for publication in the *Papeles de Nueva España* (Zavala, 1938: p. 44). While there are some references to Tepexi in the prehispanic and posthispanic sources, they are, for the most part, indirect and give only glimpses of its history.

It is not mentoned by name in the early part of the *Historia Tolteca-Chichimeca* which recounts the migration of the Nonoalca-Chichimeca from Tula in the thirteenth century. Their route took them to Huehuetlan, and then southwest toward Tepexi some twelve kilometers away. Eventually they settled to the east and south in the present states of Puebla, Oaxaca, and Veracruz (*Historia Tolteca-Chichimeca* 1947: pp. 71–75, map facing p. LXIV).

The Tolteca-Chichimeca migrants arrived in Cholula probably in A.D. 1292. After some years of domination by the resident Olmeca-Xicalanca, they revolted, and with the aid of the Chichimecs wrested Cholula from the grasp of the Olmeca-Xilcalanca, probably in 1297 (*Historia Tolteca-Chichimeca* 1947: pp. 75–86; Jiménez Moreno 1952–53: p. 313). Tepexi is not mentioned in this account, but it is worth noting that archaeological evidence places the founding of Tepexi around this time.

Around A.D. 1327 the Chichimecs moved into southern Puebla and established two domains: Quauhtinchantlaca and Totomiuaque whose capitals were at the present towns of Cuautinchán and Totimehuacán. The *Historia Tolteca-Chichimeca* recounts the formation of the two domains, but Tepexi is not named in the account. It is listed, however, as a town of the Quauhtinchantlaca domain in the note on its conquest by the Mexicans at the turn of the sixteenth century (*Historia Tolteca-Chichimeca,* 1947: pp. 114, 122). Tepeaca (Tepeyácac), which was the *cabecera* to Tepexi as well as twenty-two other towns after the region was captured by the Mexicans, was an important center in the Quauhtinchantlaca domain from the beginning. There is some indication that Tepeaca was established at this time, and from its inception it seems to have been powerful, and a rival to Quauhtinchan. Ultimately Quauhtinchan sank into oblivion and Tepeaca became important under the Mexicans (with Quauhtinchan as its subject town) and was able to maintain its dominant position under the Spaniards.

Other towns which had a relationship with Tepexi according to historical or archaeological data are listed as subject towns in the Quauhtinchantlaca domain. They are Molcaxac, Itzocan, Acatlan, Petlalzinco, and Chila (*Historia Tolteca-Chichimeca,* 1947: 60-64: pp. 102–124, passim; Barlow, 1949: pp. 100–101).

Quauhtinchan fell before the army of Tlatelolco in 10 Tochtli under the Mixtec calendrical system or 11 Tochtli under the Mexican, that is, A.D. 1438. Following the pattern of establishing political relationships by means of family ties, Tlatelolco made a number of alliances through marriages with the members of noble families of towns in southern Puebla. Tepexi was among these towns. The *Anales de Tlatelolco* records that "Mometzcopinatzin, the older sister of Coluatzin was sent to Tepexi," and the references to the birth of Quauhtlatouatzin earlier in the paragraph indicate that she was sent at the time Tlatelolco was invading this part of Puebla (*Historia Tolteca-Chichimeca,* 1947: p. 114; *Anales de Tlatelolco,* 1948: pp. 24, 53; Jiménez Moreno, 1952–1953: p. 312).

Tepeaca was conquered by the Mexicans in 13 Tochtli (A.D. 1466) during the reign of Axayacatl. A year later Acatlan fell. "In the year 11 Acatl (A.D. 1503) Tlachquiáuitl, Señor of Tepexi was defeated. The Mexicans defeated and conquered him because Ocelotzin, Señor of Quauahtlatlauhcan (Huatlatlauca) had been defeated by Tlachquiáuitl and when the Mexicans learned of the destruction of Ocelotzin, Señor of Quauahtlatlauhcan, then the Mexicans destroyed those of Tepexi" (*Anales de Tlatelolco,* 1948: p. 59; *Historia Tolteca-Chichimeca,* 1947: pp. 116, 118, 122; Jiménez Moreno, 1952–1953: p. 312).

During the reign of Ahuizotl, according to Tezozomoc (1878: cap. 76), Tepexi was among the towns which provided food and supplies to the king and army when they passed through the southern Puebla territory. These provisions were not tribute payments (see Paso y Troncoso, 1906: pp. 59–60). They may have been mandatory gifts since the marriage of Mometzcopinatzin to a member of the Tepexi ruling family linked the two centers and forced certain obligations on the smaller town. The date given for the conquest of Tepexi, A.D. 1503, was the last year of Ahuizotl's reign. If these courtesies were extended *during* his reign, as Tezozomoc seems to indicate, not just in the last year, then they were obviously the obligatory gifts of a subordinate ally. If, however, they were extended only in the last year of Ahuizotl's rule after Tepexi was conquered, they must be interpreted as additional levies, apart from tribute, borne by a defeated town.

While information on the military history of Tepexi is scant, its wars seem to have been mainly with the towns of the Mixteca Baja over tributary territory. Acatlan, Piaxtla, and Cuthá have been named specifically (Paso y Troncoso, 1906: pp. 60, 79) Cassío, 1940: pp. 27–28). However, it also had interests to the north, as the war with Huatlatlauca indicates. It is also listed with Huatlatlauca in the *Matricula de Tributos* as one of the twenty-three towns subject to Tepeaca and tributary to the Mexicans as of 1519 (Barlow, 1949: pp. 100–101). Thus it appears that Tepexi stood on the outskirts of two zones: the Puebla zone dominated by Tepeaca to the north, and the part of the Mixteca Baja dominated by Acatlan to the south.

Because of its wars with the towns of the Mixteca Baja, according to Barlow (1949: p. 101), it may have been integrated in the northern province in the interests of peace. Itzocan, also involved in wars with Acatlan, was subject to Tepeaca at this time, perhaps for the same reason. On the other hand, Piaxtla, many times at war with Acatlan, was together with it as a subject town of Yoaltepec to the south, and old enemies, Petlaltzingo and Chila, were both subject to Coixtlahuaca (Barlow, 1949: pp. 100–118). In 1580 Tepexi (with Temascalapa) was a subject town of Petlaltzingo which in turn was subject to Acatlan (Paso y Troncoso, 1906: pp. 56, 69). This new alignment may be a reflection of the postconquest population decimation in the area (Cook and Simpson, 1948; Borah and Cook, 1963), which made the consolidation of large areas necessary and forced the administrators to put aside considerations of former political enmities.

The major problem in dealing with the history of Tepexi in the sixteenth century is that at some point in the first half of the century the people from Tepexi moved from the present archaeological site (now called Tepexi el Viejo) to the site of the present town of Tepexi de Rodríguez. Excavations at Tepexi de Rodríguez have revealed Preclassic and Classic horizons (Cook de Leonard, 1953: pp. 434–435). It was probably overshadowed in the Postclassic by Tepexi el Viejo, but was undoubtedly in existence as a village. Carmen Cook de Leonard (1961: p. 91) has suggested that the move took place when the Mexican conquered the town. (She uses A.D. 1502 as the date of conquest. In this investigation A.D. 1503 is used based on the correlation by Jiménez Moreno (1952–1953).) Conquest by the Mexicans, however, did not mean annihilation of the town (the Mexicans were, after all, interested in a flourishing town which could furnish tribute), and so this is no reason to fix this date as the date of the abandonment of Tepexi el Viejo. In addition, the existence of Tlatelolco Black/Orange which dates around A.D. 1500 at Tepexi el Viejo suggests it was occupied after A.D. 1503.

In A.D. 1520 Cortés with the help of the Tlaxcallans conquered Tepexi (Mazihcatzin, 1927: p. 78). The description of the town that was conquered indicates the place was Tepexi el Viejo not Tepexi de Rodríguez. Sometime between A.D. 1520 and A.D. 1537 the population of Tepexi el Viejo moved or was moved to the little village six kilometers to the southeast and conferred upon it its own name of Tepexi which means "rocky place" or "precipitous place" in Nahuatl (Peñafiel, 1897: p. 264). The fact that Tepexi el Viejo was abandoned in these years is suggested by the lack of colonial period artifacts and by documentary evidence which places the community at the site of Tepexi de Rodríguez by A.D. 1537.

In A.D. 1537 a Marín (also Martín) Cortés upon petition to the viceroy, Antonio de Mendoza, received approval to raise 100,000 mulberry trees and develop a silk industry in the provinces of Huejotzingo, Cholula, and Tlaxcala. In return for his work he asked, in part, for Tepexi as an *encomienda* for twenty years, and he planned to cultivate 10,000 mulberry trees there (Icaza, 1928: pp. 26–27, 93–94; Borah, 1943: pp. 10–13). The silk industry was established, and within the next ten years sericulture became one of the country's most important industries. Borah (1943: p. 25) suggests that Tepexi "may have served as a center through which the silk industry was introduced . . ." into the Mixteca, a region which ultimately became the most important in the development of sericulture.

It is difficult to say when Tepexi began to be called "de la Seda." The *Relaciones* of 1580 refer to it as Tepexi (with variations) without any modifier. Torquemada (1723: p. 330), referring to events in 1576, calls it "Tepexi de la Seda," but, considering the boom of the silk industry soon after its inception, it seems likely "de la Seda" was added very soon after 1537.

The most important piece of documentary evidence available on Tepexi is a painted tribute record in the collection of the Museum of the American Indian, Heye Foundation, New York, that has been carefully analyzed by Carmen Cook de Leonard (1961). She suggests that it is a nineteenth-century copy of a sixteenth-century manuscript, and that the original may have been drawn for Marín Cortés during his stay at Tepexi as an indication of the tribute he could expect from the town. The following translation is after Carmen Cook de Leonard (1961: pp. 87–90).

"Don Gonzalo Mazatzin, Chief Ruler and native Lord of Tepexic de la Seda and of its subject 'Barrios' and land properties, and the tribute they paid him before the Spaniards arrived, is the following. First Trinal part of the year." The names over the tribute objects are: "Slaves; Golden Jewels; Precious Stones; Fine Feathers; Cloth, plain and with designs; Loin Cloth; Skirts; Blouses; Cloths; [Cacao]; Hens [probably turkeys]; Sandals; Chairs; Rattles; Calabash, Wooden or Earthen vessels; Bowls; Calabash, Wooden or Earthen Vessels; Pots; Pitchers." On the next line is "Don Juan Moctesuma" and "The Marquis of the Valley" with drawings of individuals. Under "Second Trinal part" are tribute objects depicted without identifying Spanish names. Under "Third Trinal part" is another row of unnamed tribute objects as well as under "Fourth

Trinal part." The inscription on the right side reads: "The non-irrigated lands were worked by the people from Tepexic every year for the maintenance of said Lords." In the upper frame is written "And every twenty days, on their turn, said town of Tepexic gave a hundred and twenty Indians, and the same amount of women for the service of the House, and they would bring in acknowledgment of the said lords the following things." The tribute objects are drawn and named. They are "Cacao, Hens [probably turkeys], Grinding Women, *Axi* [dried peppers], Salt, Beans, Squash seeds, Deer, Rabbits. In acknowledgment the people from Tepexic would assist (and) the said Lords for their services every twenty days with dishes, that were necessary." Below the frame is written "They would arrange plots every year in irrigated lands of these four things." In the bottom frame is written and depicted "Cotton, Maize, Pumpkins, Hot Peppers."

The three individuals mentioned in the tribute record cannot be identified with certainty. However, the picture of Don Gonzalo Mazatzin in which he is shown in prehispanic clothes and on a prehispanic throne, the depiction of his name glyph, and the phrase "before the Spaniards arrived" all argue for the interpretation that the tribute list was given to a prehispanic Tepexi, and that the term "Tepexi de la Seda" is an anachronism, probably added years after the pictographs were made as a translation of the glyph.

The term "Señor natural" indicates that Don Gonzalo Mazatzin was an Indian ruler who was the legitimate and hereditary heir to his throne because he was in a direct line of succession from native rulers. A resident "Señor natural" indicates that the center had the political structure to control a zone of subject hamlets. These subject hamlets acknowledged the right of the lord to exercise control over them. The population of the center and the hamlets were referred to collectively as the people of Tepexi whether they lived at the center and worked irrigated lands or in distant hamlets tilling non-irrigated soil. The main body of the tribute record, however, seems to deal with tribute received as a result of conquest. Each trinal part line begins with the drawing of slaves. That these slaves are war captives can be seen by the collar linking their necks and by their bound hands. Figures depicted in this way have been identified commonly in the documentary sources as war captives. Don Gonzalo Mazatzin may have been the lord of Tepexi at the time of the Conquest. Perhaps it was he who moved the population of Tepexi el Viejo to the present site.

The other individuals in the record were probably from the immediate postconquest period. Don Juan Moctesuma may have been a successor to Don Gonzalo Mazatzin. The "Marquis of the Valley" identified by a picture of Hernan Cortés is undoubtedly Marín Cortés who was called Hernando Marín Cortés (Icaza, 1928: pp. 26–27, 93–94), and whose name may have caused him to be confused with the conqueror.

In summary, the documentary evidence suggests that Tepexi was important in the fifteenth century, and probably before, as part of the Quauhtinchantlaca domain. The Tlatelolcos felt it was to their advantage to arrange a marriage with its ruling family. Its tribute record shows it had an integrated zone of subject hamlets as well as a conquered tributary territory and indicates that the population subject to Tepexi was large. However, population size and density are difficult to determine from the record because it does not give amounts or other numbers which might help calculate the population to any extent. Its tributary territory was a source of conflict with such centers as Acatlan, Huatlatlauca, and Piaztla. Thus, it had connections with both the Mixteca Baja and Puebla. (This is borne out by the archaeological record.) Tepexi, then, emerges from the fragmentary documentary evidence as a middling Postclassic community in the Mixteca-Puebla region with an active military-political history marked by continuing conquests and defeats. In this it probably mirrors the history of most of the middle-size and large communities throughout the region.

ANTIQUARIAN AND ARCHAEOLOGICAL REPORTS ON TEPEXI

In 1807 G. Dupaix, the indefatigable explorer, visited Tepexi and wrote:

My curiosity was gratified by the sight of the several ruins which I discovered in that neighborhood. The first that attracted my attention was a massy pile of building apparently designed for the defense of some interior structure. This work exhibits a system of fortification which I cannot persuade myself was ever known to the inhabitants of the Old Continent. The walls are constructed of square stones, cemented with a durable mortar composed of lime and sand and presents an elevation which gradually recedes from base to summit, forming a series of overhanging platforms [of which there are eight] . . .

The space which this building covers is immense, but its situation precluded the possibility of any accurate admeasurement. It stands on the projecting angle of rock surrounded by vast precipices, [and protected by] innumerable serpents, fostered by a climate so intensely hot as that of the Lower Misteca. . . . The buildings which form the interior of this vast structure are disposed with such order and regularity, as to lead me to imagine that they were once the residence of some potent Indian prince; for notwithstanding its present state of dilapidation and decay, the traces of arrangement and design in the disposition of its several parts are clearly visible, while the whole building must have been executed with rule, compass, and level or some instruments of a corresponding nature. (Kingsborough, 1831–1848: not paginated.)

The site apparently went unnoticed for more than one hundred years. It is said that in the first half of the twentieth century pottery from Tepexi was brought to Cholula and sold there as Cholula Polychrome from Cholula. In November of 1949 the site was sacked badly and in December of that year Jorge Obregon de la Parra, an employee of the Instituto Nacional de

Antropología e Historia, went to the site to report on the damage and make what repairs he could. His report, dated January 9, 1950, describes the site briefly and gives a short account of the pottery and stone artifacts he collected from the surface. He notes that the site appeared to him to be more of a fortress than an urban or ceremonial center and reports on the existence of plazas on different levels and habitations. He found the pottery similar to that of Cholula (Cholulteca), Acatlan, and Itzocan particularly, but it seemed to him to be of the Mixteca-Puebla horizon in general. He also mentions "Aztec III types." He found points and blades, and an ear-plug of obsidian, a small axe, a *penate* of a green stone, beads of jade and white stone, and some small worked shells (Obregon de la Parra, 1950).

In 1951 Pedro Armillas (1951: p. 80) described Tepexi as a hill-fort site and, following an unidentified source, as having moats and a bastion with loopholes. Carmen Cook de Leonard (1953: pp. 438–439) describes it as a fortress. In addition, she points out the existence of a palace, pyramidal structures, and a number of buildings. She dug a stratigraphic pit, but the analysis is not published. However, she has noted that her study of the pottery indicates that the site was founded in the thirteenth century (Cook de Leonard, 1961: p. 91). In 1964 I visited Tepexi as part of a survey of military sites in the Central Mexican and adjacent regions and published a brief descripton (Gorenstein, 1966*b*: p. 67).

Fig. 2. The main precinct.

Thus, there has been very little archaeological work at Tepexi which can be used as a background to this study. The discussion of the prehistory of Tepexi el Viejo must perforce be based primarily on the work of the present expedition.

ARCHITECTURE

Tepexi el Viejo stands on a hill which is surrounded on three sides by deep canyons. There is a main pre-

Fig. 1. The main precinct and subsites.

Map 3. Map of the main precinct of Tepexi. Cia. Mexicana Aerofoto S.A.

cinct and five other areas of occupation which are designated Subsites I, II, III, IV, and V (figs. 1 and 2).

The main precinct of Tepexi contains a number of building complexes and mounds and is completely enclosed by a series of massive outer walls (maps 3 and 4). There are five sectors on different levels within the main precinct (figs. 3 and 4). The difference in height between adjacent levels is more than 6 meters in one case and as little as 1.5 meters. The levels were built up to the desired grade by means of layers of roughly shaped pieces of caliche measuring up to 0.65 to 0.75 meter in length and width, and rarely more than 0.15 meter in thickness. The pieces were laid down apparently in a wet adobe mixture containing sherds, worked and unworked stone, and small pieces of caliche in successive horizontal planes. In a test excavation in Sector C, six successive layers of caliche were uncovered in about one meter of depth.

There is a general stylistic uniformity in the construc-

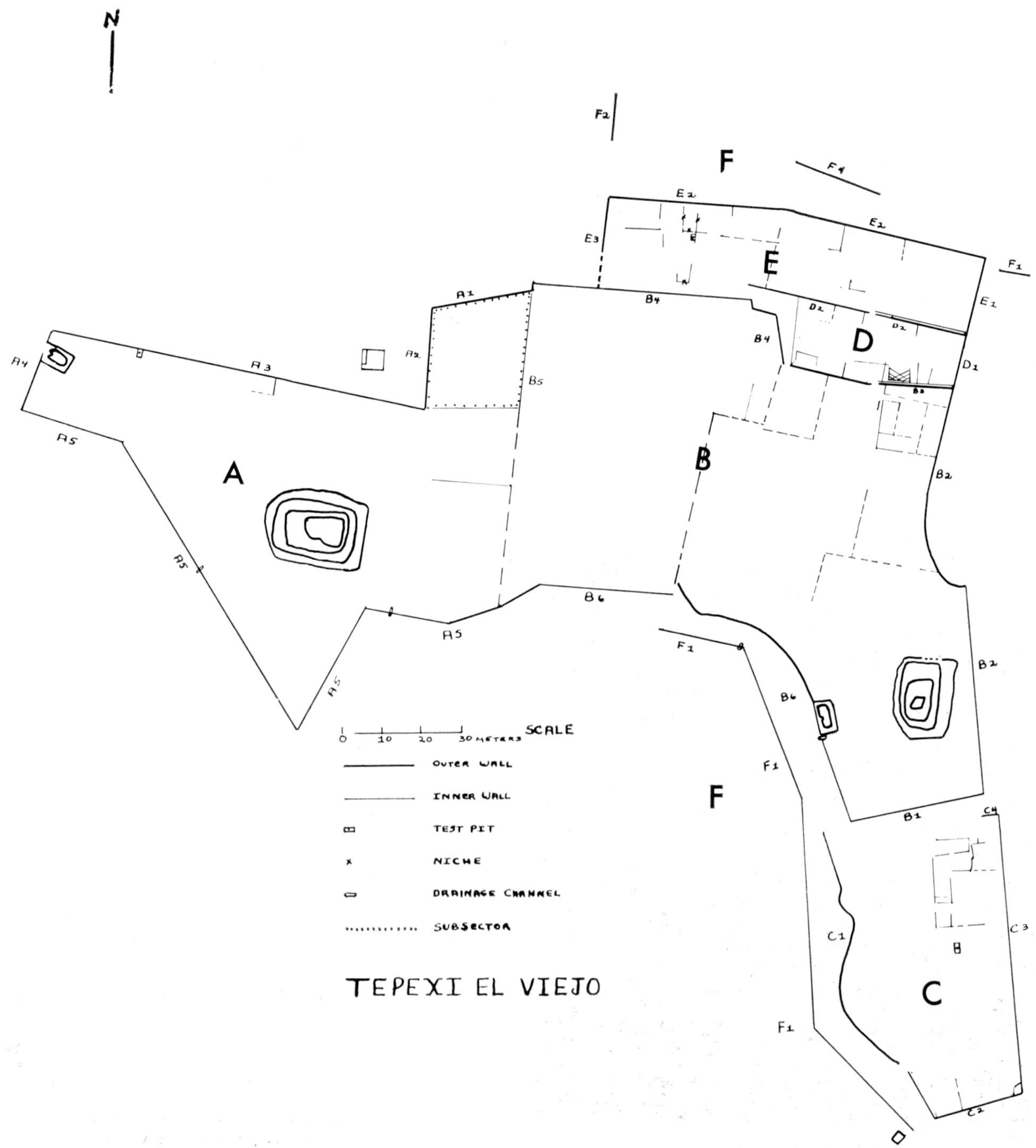

MAP 4. Plan of the main precinct of Tepexi.

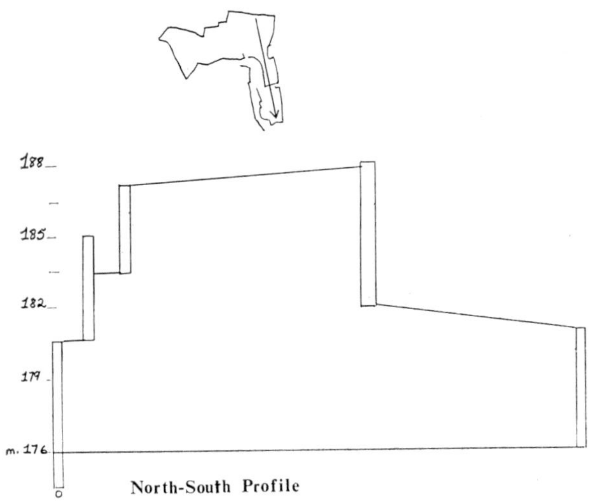

FIG. 3. North-south profile of main precinct.

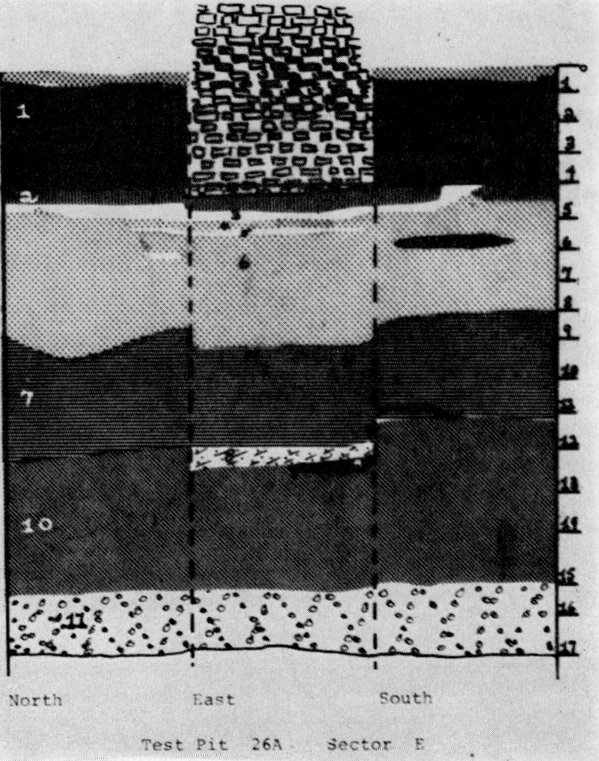

FIG. 5. Stratigraphy of test pit in Sector E.

tion technique at Tepexi. The core of walls was made of irregularly shaped caliche blocks set in the wet adobe mixture containing sherds, rocks, and caliche (fig. 6). A facing of shaped caliche blocks set in the same kind of mortar was added. The horizontal and vertical (outer and side) faces of these blocks were trimmed, sometimes only roughly, other times carefully. Viewed in the wall they appear to be parallelepipeds. They are, however, wedged-shaped, that is, long and tapered toward the back which enabled them to slip easily into the mortar and hold. The facing was sometimes covered with a lime plaster which is so thin, it more properly may be called a washcoat (fig. 7) (Littman, 1957: p. 136). However, it was probably sufficient to protect what is essentially a fragile facing construction from the incursions of rainwater.

Courses are overlapping for the most part. The great vertical fissures in one wall (C-wall-2) may be due to the lack of overlapping in this wall which weakened its structure. Small apertures in the lower courses of the walls, measuring from 0.5 to 0.7 meter in width and 0.3 to 0.5 meter in length, and 0.5 to 0.7

meter in depth, may have been used to hold wooden supports for planks on which the mason stood to set the upper courses. On the high walls there were successive groups of these.

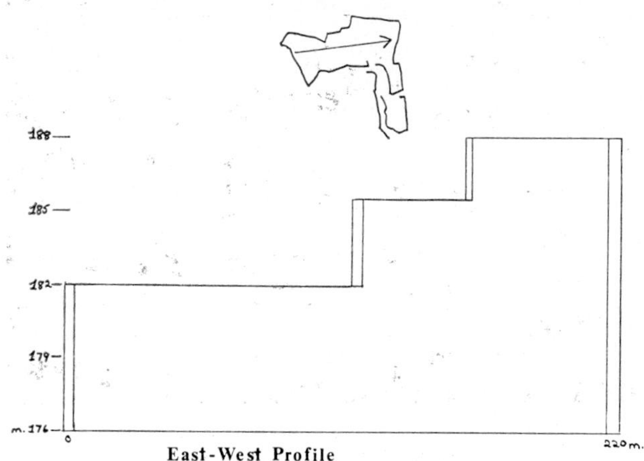

FIG. 4. East-west profile of main precinct.

FIG. 6. Wall construction showing inner aggregate of adobe mixed with sherds, rocks, and caliche and the cut caliche blocks of the façade wedged in it. B-Wall-5.

Fig. 7. Example of plaster coating over caliche blocks.
Sector E.

Outside corners were constructed by using large caliche blocks with carefully cut right-angle faces. Joints were not always attempted. Two walls were sometimes constructed so that they met, even touched, but they were not bonded.

The caliche used in the wall and the underground construction is found at the site but may have been brought in also. A possible quarry is one-half kilo-meter north-northwest of the site. The caliche used in all construction is laminar and breaks into tabular blocks. A simple percussion technique was probably used to form the blocks into the desired size and shape, and subsequent abrading does not seem to have been done.

Within the style there is a range in the manner in which the blocks were cut, the uniformity of block size and shape, and in the evenness of the courses. The extremes of the range are represented by one variant in which the blocks are roughly hewn, irregular in shape, and the courses are haphazard (fig. 8); and by a refined variant in which the blocks show careful trimming, are nearly the same size and shape, and set in even courses (fig. 9). The rougher style variants are found in the sectors built earlier (Sector A, B, C), and only the refined forms seem to have been used in later constructions (Sectors D and E). These variations, however, should not be interpreted as distinct styles. There is a definite stylistic unity in the architecture at Tepexi.

In some places walls have been repaired or rebuilt, and the method of construction is different from the Tepexi style. In these cases, instead of a mud mortar, small pebbles have been used between the large caliche blocks. This method is known to be both prehispanic (at Coixtlahuaca, for example) and posthispanic. Because at this site it is associated with definite posthispanic features, it has been assumed that this style was used at Tepexi after it had been abandoned in the sixteenth century.

Fig. 8. Example of the rough variant of architectural style.
C-Wall-2.

Fig. 9. Example of the refined variant of architectural style.
Sector E building complex.

There are four main types of construction in the main zone: broad plaza areas, pyramidal platforms, mounds with recesses, building complexes, and outer walls.

There were probably two large plazas at Tepexi with a portion of their floors, at least, covered with plaster. They were, very likely, used in part as the sites for markets (Dahlgren, 1954: p. 241) and for civic and ceremonial functions.

The mounds were not uncovered in this investigation. However, an examination of pothunters' holes trenched through the mounds and cleared surfaces indicates that the mounds were constructed of irregularly shaped caliche blocks set in a wet adobe mixture containing sherds, stone, and caliche, and faced with caliche blocks with sharp edges and straight faces. There are two distinct varieties: the larger mounds which are in the plazas appear to be pyramidal platforms; the smaller mounds are set on the top of the outer walls and have small recesses on the outside face.

Building complexes are subdivided into units. There is no difference in the construction between the outside walls and the inside walls. They are invariably no more than 0.8 meter in width and carefully cut caliche blocks were used in the facing. The blocks measured from 0.2 to 0.3 meter in length and 0.05 to 0.1 meter in width. In some cases they were covered with a fine lime plaster or washcoat. Some of the outside walls of the building complexes have run-offs made of plaster to lead rainwater from the roofs to the ground. There are niches in four inside walls of one complex. There is no sufficient indication of the height of the walls or the character of the roofs. The complexes were placed near the edge of the hill and the great outer walls built along the hillslope were extended upward to form at least one outside wall. They may have been the apartments of the noble family of Tepexi and civic structures (*cf.* Dahlgren, 1954: pp. 133–136).

The outer walls are built against the hillslope. Layered caliche has been used in some places to build up the surface of the hill. For the most part these walls do not rise above the floor level of the sector, rather the top course of caliche blocks, that is, the finished top of the wall, is even with the floor of the sector. Only where the outer walls have been extended to form an outside wall of a building complex do they rise above the surface of the sector. There are also low walls, measuring 0.6 to 1 meter high, which seem to have been built after Tepexi was abandoned. The outer walls measure more than 1.5 meters in depth, and are as high as 15 meters. The caliche blocks used in the outer walls are larger than those in the building walls. They measure up to 1 meter in length and width and generally around 0.15 meter in depth, although some are between 0.15 and 0.3 meter. The walls slant inward from base to top at approximately 10° off the vertical or have a vestigial

talud-tablero articulation. In the last there is an inwardly sloping bottom wall, a slight indentation, and then an upper section which continues to slope inward. Channels were built inside the walls and probably were used for drainage. They led the water from the surface of the sectors through the walls and out along the hillslopes.

Because the site has been only partly cleared and is somewhat ruined, measurements cannot be absolutely correct. Every effort has been made to give the measurements of the functioning architecture and not the ruins. This report, however, lacks the description of those architectural features which can be revealed only by extensive excavation. But since the site is in good condition and not excessively overgrown, the major features can be set down with some assurance.

The designations used are merely to facilitate description and do not have a reality of their own. For example, if two designations are used for a continuing wall, it does not mean there is a break in the construction of the wall. The reader should use the designations only to locate features on the plan and rely on the prose description for an account of the character of the features.

SECTOR A

Sector A is in the westernmost part of the main precinct, immediately to the east of Sector B. It is about 119 meters in the east-west direction, and ranges from nearly 22 meters to 82 meters in the north-south direction. Test excavations in this sector show that it was built up by layers of caliche. In certain parts of the sector the floor is covered by a thin plaster, and it is likely the entire floor of this sector was plastered. Much of Sector A appears to have constituted a plaza area.

Other test excavations revealed burials in the western part of the sector, but they were badly disturbed by pothunters, and it is no longer possible to determine burial procedures or the character of the graves. There were no associated artifacts, merely the sherds and worked stone of the fill. It is possible that these burials were immediately postconquest.

In the northeast part of Sector A is a subsector. It is outside the outer wall of Sector B which is its eastern boundary, but it is enclosed within the outer walls of Sector A which are its northern and western boundaries. Its southern boundary is a low wall about 1.5 meters high and 24 meters from north to south and nearly 23 meters from east to west.

There is another low wall about 1.5 meters high, some 17 meters to the south and parallel to the southern wall of the subsector. It may be the wall of a building complex.

About 5.3 meters south of the northern boundary of this sector is a shallow platform about 0.15 meter high running about 5.6 meters from east to west. The facing is made of carefully cut caliche blocks with sharp edges and straight faces, and is covered with a thin coat of lime plaster.

MOUNDS

There are two mounds in Sector A. The smaller lies on the westernmost point of the sector and of the main zone. Its western face is on a line with the upper section of the outer wall and has the vestiges of a small recess. The mound measures 6 meters from east to west and 4.6 meters from north to south. It is now 1.5 meters high.

The second mound is larger and occupies a central place in the plaza. It measures 24 meters in the east-west direction and 18 meters from north to south. There may be a stairway on the north face. It is probably a pyramidal platform. The facing blocks are parallel-epipeds, are not carefully made, and the courses are uneven (fig. 10).

OUTER WALLS

A-Wall-1 which runs for 24 meters appears to continue B-Wall-4, but it turns from the east-west direction of B-Wall-4 to the south for about 3 meters and then it continues in a general east-west direction for 24 meters. It was about 4 meters in height. A-Wall-2, 23 meters long, is not at a right angle to A-Wall-1 and is now almost entirely broken down. However, it appears to have been the same height as A-Wall-1. A-Wall-3 is at a right angle to A-Wall-2 and runs east-west for 92 meters. Its height was 4.6 meters. These three walls form the northern boundary of the main precinct as well as the sector. A-Wall-4 runs north and south for 20 meters and marks the western border of Sector A and the main precinct. It was 6 meters high. It is in good condition unlike the other outer walls of Sector A, and its profile can be described. It has an inwardly sloping lower section, then an indentation of 0.25 meter, and an inwardly sloping upper section. A-Wall-5 marks the entire southern border of Sector A and part of the southern border of the

FIG. 11. Recess in small mound in Sector B.

FIG. 12. Outer wall A-Wall-s.

FIG. 10. Mound in Sector A which is probably a pyramidal platform.

main precinct. It is 173 meters long, and its most striking feature is the sharp Z outline at the portion of the sector where the large mound stands. A-Wall-5 has five (and may have had eight) indented sections (fig. 12). At this point the wall is 15 meters high. The rest of the wall is broken down in most places, but at no point was it probably less than 5 meters in height. The caliche blocks which constitute the facings of the outer walls of Sector A are roughly shaped and the courses are even. The exception is the Z-shaped portion of A-Wall-5 which suggests that this part of the wall was built or rebuilt at another time, and the more refined style used.

DRAINAGE CHANNELS

There are two channels in A-Wall-5 which run from the surface of the sector through the length of the wall at a 45° angle. The opening on the sector surface of the westernmost drainage channel in Sector A measures 0.8 by 0.7 meter and is 1.35 meters from the edge of the wall. The channel east of it measures 0.4 by 0.6 meter and is also about 1.35 meters from the edge of the outer wall. Its opening at the bottom of the wall is 1.5 meters high and about 0.4 meter wide. Both the floor and the roof of the channel are finished with long steeply overlapping caliche blocks, and the inner side walls are faced. These channels may have been used to divert water runoff from the northern part of the site.

SECTOR B

Sector B is the highest level of the main precinct. It is viewed as one sector although there is a low rise in the center which puts the western part more than 2 meters below the eastern for a distance of 41 meters. For about 5 meters one can follow the remains of a low 1.5 meter wall on the extreme southern end which is built against the hillslope or side. Its facing is gone. It is continuous with an outer wall of Sector B (B-Wall-6), and, for this reason, it and the rise might have been used as a sector boundary dividing Sector B into two sectors. But because for 26 meters along this line the two parts are on the same level, it was decided to designate the parts as one sector and to note simply the difference in elevation. The western section shows no remains of walls, and may have been a plaza. No plastered floors were uncovered, however. The eastern section has been potted badly, and some walls razed.

The sector measures from about 64 to 102 meters from north to south to 35 to 100 meters from east to west. It lies immediately to the east of Sector A and may at one time have been partly continuous with it. It is now separated from it on the northern part of its western boundary by an outer wall. However, the southern part of the western boundary is only a low wall about 1.5 meters high. There is easy passage here between the two sectors. Sector B is immediately to the north and connects to it by a passageway. It is separated from Sector C, which is directly to the south, by an outer wall.

BUILDING COMPLEXES

There is one major building complex in this sector; it lies in the northeast corner. As a whole, it measures about 15 meters square. The northern wall of this complex is the upward extension of an outer wall built against the hillslope or side of the northern border of Sector B before Sector D was added. This is also true of the eastern wall which is an extension of B-Wall-2. The western and southern walls of this building complex are free-standing. About 1 meter west of the western wall of the complex and parallel to it are the remains of a wall running 3.7 meters and now about 0.5 meter high. The inner walls of the complex divide it into five units. The facing blocks of the walls have sharp edges and straight surfaces and the courses are even.

The remains of a small building complex are found about 34 meters to the west of the west wall of the larger complex. Only 3 meters of its south wall, now 2 meters high, and 9 meters of its east wall are standing. The facing is the same as in the large complex.

A number of other walls were located in this sector, but it was not possible to determine their function without further excavation. They are noted on the plan. They are of the same stylistic variation as the two building complexes of this sector.

MOUNDS

There are two mounds in Sector B. The larger lies 14 meters to the north of the sector's southern border and 4.6 meters west of its eastern. It measures almost 20 meters from north to south and 15 meters from east to west and is nearly 4 meters high. Test excavation of the south side revealed a straight façade. The facing blocks do not have very sharp edges or straight faces, nor are the courses very even. It is probably a pyramidal platform.

The second mound is on the top of the western wall (B-Wall-2) of the sector, 20 meters north of the southern border. It is 8 meters from north to south, 5.5 meters from east to west and 2 meters above the level of the sector. In the west face of this mound is a small recess (fig. 11). It is about 1.3 meters deep, measures 1.4 meters across, and is 1.5 meters high. The recess has a facing of caliche blocks that are variable in size and have irregular surfaces. They were covered with a thin plaster. This mound is similar to the westernmost mound in Sector A. Both are small, sit directly on top of an outer wall, and have a small recess on the outside face.

OUTER WALLS

B-Wall-1 forms the southern border of the sector. It extends 32 meters. It slopes inward from base to top 10° off the vertical, and may have been as many as

10 meters high. The facing blocks are not carefully trimmed, nor of the same size; however, the courses are even.

B-Wall-2 is a continuation of B-Wall-1 and runs approximately north and south forming the eastern border of the sector. Its construction is the same as B-Wall-1. It was probably 6 meters high. It follows the natural contour of the hillslope, running 49 meters in a north-south direction, turning west with the hillslope for 3 meters, and then continuing north for another 49 meters. It was built above the surface of the sector only in the area of the building complex where it forms the east wall of the complex. There is no break in the courses of the wall at that point, so it is impossible to tell from the outside courses where it leaves the hillslope or side and becomes free-standing. The slope, however, is not continued above the surface where the free-standing wall is vertical.

B-Wall-3 forms a sharp right angle with B-Wall-2 and is the northern border of the sector. It rises nearly 5 meters above the floor of the sector to the north of it, but only 3.5 meters are against the hillslope or side. The upper 1.5 meters form the north wall of the main building complex of Sector B. The wall runs for some 18 meters, then is interrupted by a passageway, and continues another 19 meters, but set back to the south about 2 meters. The northeast section of the wall has a sloping lower portion, a 0.2-meter indentation, and an upper portion that continues to slope inward. The rest of the wall slopes inward 10° off the vertical in an unbroken line. The facing of this wall is of the refined variation of the Tepexi style. At the westernmost point there is a second passageway that leads from Sector E to Sector B.

The west wall of the latter passageway is the beginning of B-Wall-4 (fig. 13). It runs north-south for 11 meters, turns west for 6 meters and north for 1.5 meters. It continues west to the end of Sector B, a distance of 51 meters. Its last 15 meters forms part of the northern border of the main precinct. Its height

Fɪɢ. 14. Outer wall B-Wall-4.

was probably nearly 8 meters. It is built entirely against the hillslope or side, and its top is even with the surface of Sector B. The portion of the wall which is part of the passageway has an unbroken inwardly sloping outline; the section to the west, however, has a sloping base, and indentation of 0.25 meter and an upper section which continues the inward slope. The facing is of the fine variety.

B-Wall-5 is a continuation of B-Wall-4 to the south for 29 meters. It is nearly 5 meters high for the most part. In style it is the same as B-Wall-4 except it does not have the talud-tablero effect; rather it has an unbroken profile line, sloping inwardly. It marks the northwest boundary of Sector B, and is also the eastern boundary of the subsector in Sector A.

The remaining 46 meters of the western boundary of Sector B is now a gradual rise between Sectors A and B. It is not possible to determine the juncture between the rise and B-Wall-5, but it is clear that a low wall stood between Sectors A and B for at least part of the 46 meters. An exposed section of this wall, 1.5 meters long and 0.75 meter high, has a finely done facing and is covered in part with lime plaster.

B-Wall-6 is the southwestern boundary of Sector B. It extends for 42 meters before it turns south for another 71 meters. Much of the southern part of the wall has broken down. An 11-meter section has been rebuilt in modern times with prehistoric blocks. It follows the ancient wall contour. The western part is separated from the southern by the rise of land within Sector B. It was probably about 8 meters high. It connects to B-Wall-1, but its masonry is of the finer variant and was covered with a plaster.

CHANNEL

There is a channel in B-Wall-6, 20 meters north of B-Wall-1, and directly to the south of the small mound. It extends from the top of Sector B about 1.5 meters to its base in the face of the wall. The channel is at least 1 meter deep in some places, but it has been potted, and its exact dimensions cannot be given without excavation. This channel, unlike the others described above, is not inside the wall. Rather the wall turns inward in two places, about 1 meter apart, to form the sides of the channel. There is, thus, no outside wall, and the channel appears as a three-sided sloping recess. There is some question as to whether it was used for drainage.

SECTOR C

Sector C is the southernmost sector of the main precinct, and lies directly to the south of Sector B. Between the two sectors is an area measuring 4.6 meters from north to south on the eastern end. In the center and western end of the 4.6 meter wide area is an accumulation of rubber, soil, and vegetation which would cover over any wall that might be on the northwest boundary of Sector C. Nevertheless, B-Wall-1 clearly marks the southern boundary of Sector B, and there is no direct passage from Sector C to Sector B.

The surface of Sector C is about 8 meters below the surface of Sector B, and 5 meters above the surface just outside its southern wall. A test trench revealed that this sector had been built up to its present level by successive layers of caliche blocks (fig. 14). The sector measures 65 meters from north to south, and as many as 40 meters from east to west. The building up of the surface level of this sector appears to be contemporary with the construction of C-Wall-2. On the southern boundary there is a wall which rises from 1 to 2 meters above the surface of the sector. It is an upwards continuation of the outer wall, C-Wall-2. The same is true of the eastern boundary where the outer wall, C-Wall-3, rises up to a meter in some places above the sector surface.

BUILDING COMPLEX

There is one building complex in Sector C (fig. 15). It stands in the northeast corner of the sector. It seems likely, to judge from the other building complexes, that its eastern wall was a continuation upward of the outer wall, but it is no longer extant. The outer wall, C-Wall-4, on the northeast provides an outside wall for the complex for about 4 meters. However, it is possible that the inner walls now related to C-Wall-4 were built after Tepexi was abandoned, and the outer wall never served as an outside wall for the complex. Certainly it did not serve in the northwest part of the complex where a runoff on the free-standing wall indicates it was the outside wall of the complex. The western wall is free-standing. The complex measures

Fig. 15. Building complex. Sector C.

20 meters from north to south and 14 meters from east to west, and can be divided into five units excluding the northeast corner which may be the result of modern building. The walls of the units do not always meet in bonded corners, but rather stand as separate entities that touch. The blocks of the walls are not as carefully made as those of the other building complexes. Their faces and edges are somewhat uneven, and they are irregular in size and shape. An effort was made, however, to keep the courses even by using mortar to compensate for the lack of length and width in the small blocks.

RUNOFFS

There are three runoffs. A runoff is a shallow trough of plaster on the outside of a wall which carries

Fig. 14. Test pit showing successive layers of caliche slabs which were used to build up the level of Sector C.

Fig. 16. Runoff on wall of Sector C building complex.

rain from the roof off the building at that particular place. They are the length of the wall and about 0.8 meter wide. Two are on the western wall of the complex, and one is on the northwestern free-standing wall (fig. 16).

OTHER STRUCTURES

At the southern end of the sector are two structures: an enclosure and a ramp. The enclosure is in the southeast corner and has the ground plan of a quarter of a circle which is formed by the right angles of the eastern and southern outer walls which continue above the ground level here about 1 meter and completed by an arc of caliche blocks that have been piled on each other without being set in mortar. It measures 1.6 meters in each direction. It seems possible, even probable, that this structure is not prehispanic since its manner of construction is different from the standard construction style at the site.

In the southwest corner is a platform ramp. It measures 7.6 meters from north to south and 6 meters from east to west. It rises from the ground level of the sector to the top of the outer wall which is about 2 meters above the ground level. The sides of the ramp platform meet the continuation of the outer wall at right angles, that is, the ramp platform is built directly against the continuation of the outer wall above the level of the sector. The caliche blocks used in the facing were roughly hewn, of irregular size and shape, and the courses are haphazard.

OUTER WALLS

C-Wall-1 is on the western boundary of Sector C where it runs about 79 meters from northwest to southeast following the natural contour of the hillslope. The northern part of this wall is largely fallen to rubble, and without excavation it is not possible to determine its exact relationship to B-Wall-1 and B-Wall-6 or to F-Wall-1 (see below). The facing is gone for the most part, and it is possible to say only that it was not of the fine variety.

Entranceway: Despite the poor condition of C-Wall-1, it possible to discern the remains of an entranceway about 13 meters north of its southern end. It is about 3 meters wide, but in such ruin that it cannot be described further.

C-Wall-2 is the southern border of the sector and the main precinct. It articulates with C-Wall-1 and runs from east to west about 21 meters. It was 6 meters high. Its construction is unusual for this site. The facing is split into 9 vertical sections, and there are gaps between the sections of 8 or 10 centimeters. The facing itself is made of caliche blocks whose faces are very irregular. The size and shape of these blocks vary enormously from nearly a meter in length to a few centimeters, and in width from 0.5 meter to a few centimeters. There is some attempt at courses, but since

the blocks are so varied in size and shape, the courses could not be maintained for any length. The great fissures in this wall may be due to an earthquake which split the wall where the courses did not overlap. However, it is possible that the wall simply was built poorly, and gave way at its weakest structural points. Unlike the other walls in the main precinct, it does not slope inward, rather, its face is at a right angle with its base. It was built before C-Wall-1 and C-Wall-3. It is clear architecturally that these two walls were added to C-Wall-2.

C-Wall-3 is the eastern boundary of Sector C and the main precinct, and extends 65 meters from north to south. It was made continuous with and is at right angles to C-Wall-2, but is different from it in construction. The caliche blocks of the facing have fairly even surfaces and the courses are straight. It has the gentle inward slope of many of the other walls, and is about 5 meters high. It follows a remarkably straight line, that is, it does not meander or abruptly change direction.

C-Wall-4 is continuous with C-Wall-3, and runs from east to west at right angles to it. Less than 5 meters of its length remain. It was about 3.5 meters high. The facing blocks were carefully trimmed to uniform sizes and shapes, set in even courses, and covered with plaster.

SECTOR D

Sector D lies in the northeastern part of the main zone to the north of Sector B and about 4.5 meters below it. It is essentially rectangular in shape, and measures from 12.5 to 14 meters from north to south and 40 meters from east to west.

BUILDING COMPLEX

Sector D constitutes a single building complex. The southeast wall of the complex is built directly against an outer wall of Sector B (B-Wall-3), and the southwest wall is B-Wall-3 itself. Its western wall is the east wall of the passageway that leads from Sector E to Sector B, and its northern wall is a continuation above the surface of an outer wall of the sector, as is its eastern wall (D-Wall-2 and D-Wall-1, respectively, see below). It can be divided into eight units, and excavation would undoubtedly reveal others. The refined variation of masonry was used.

PIPE

Beneath the floor of one of the units in the southeast of the sector is a pipe which appears to come from Sector B above. In the wall the pipe is roofed and floored with caliche blocks set in mortar. However, beyond the wall, the pipe is made of clay and covered with plaster. It extends up at an angle of about 20° and is rectangular in shape, measuring 0.3 meter in one direction and 0.4 meter in the other.

PLATFORM

To the west of the unit with the pipe is a platform measuring 5 meters from north to south and 5.5 meters from east to west. It is now about 1 meter high. It is of the refined stylistic variation.

PASSAGEWAYS

There are two passageways in this sector: one leads to Sector B and the other leads to Sector E. The first is *L*-shaped and is in the center of B-Wall-3. It measures 10 meters in the east-west direction and nearly 4 meters from north to south. It rises some 5 meters from the ground level of Sector D to the ground level of Sector B by means either of a ramp or stairway with shallow steps.

The second passageway is in D-Wall-2, and is merely an opening in the wall. Either a ramp or stairway led down the 3 meters to the ground level of Sector E. The opening in the wall is 1.6 meters, and the blocks at either side of the opening are placed at a 45° angle to the wall.

OUTER WALLS

D-Wall-1 is the eastern boundary of the sector, and forms part of the eastern boundary of the main precinct. It runs almost 13 meters from north to south and is continuous with B-Wall-2, that is, there is no break or interruption in the courses. However, it is perfectly clear from the outside where Sector B ends and Sector D begins since the top of D-Wall-1 is lower because Sector D is 4.5 meters below Sector B. Despite the difference in elevation between the two sectors, D-Wall-1 is about 4.5 meters high. This is because its base is on lower ground than the base of B-Wall-2. It is built against the hillslope or side, and the lower 2 meters appear to have been built first, and then sometime later the upper courses were added. The wall rises more than 1 meter above the ground level of Sector D where it forms the eastern wall of the building complex, although there is no indication of this from the outside courses. It slopes gently inward from base to the ground level of the sector where it becomes vertical. The facing is the same as B-Wall-2, that is, the blocks are not carefully cut, nor uniform in size, but the courses are even.

D-Wall-2 is the northern boundary of the sector and lies between Sectors D and E. It is at right angles with D-Wall-1 and extends 40 meters in an east-west direction. It is built against the hillslope or side and is from 3.5 to 4.5 meters high. It is highest in the eastern section, where it appears to have been built in two parts. The bottom 2 meters were built first, and then, some time later, the upper courses were added. In cross-section the bottom part of the wall slopes inward and the upper half is vertical. It is built against the hillslope or built-up side except for the upper 1.5 meters which are free-standing and form the northern wall of

the building complex of Sector D. The facing is of the refined variety.

Because of the addition of courses to the walls in Sector B combined with the consistently used refined style of facing masonry in the building complex, it seems clear that Sector D was built after Sector B and probably after Sectors A and C as well.

SECTOR E

Sector E is in the northeast corner of the main precinct, and measures from 18 to 21 meters from north to south and 89 meters from east to west. It lies directly to the north of Sector D and is 2.5 meters below its ground level. It is also to the north of Sector B and there is a 4.5 difference in elevation between the level of Sector B and the level of Sector E below it.

BUILDING COMPLEX

Like Sector D, Sector E constitutes a building complex (fig. 17). It can be divided into at least twelve units. The flooring which measured 1.6 centimeters thick was uncovered 60 centimeters below surface. Dr. Malde describes it as "Coarse sand and fine gravel in calcareous matrix (perhaps pulverized caliche); does not disaggregate in water but matrix dissolves in 1:5 HCl with rapid effervescence; floor surface white (10 YR 8/2, dry). May have been mixed as a slurry, then spread wet enough to puddle at top, and finally allowed to dry. After drying, this mixture would be difficult to decompose and would be rather durable." At 192 centimeters below surface successive layers of caliche blocks showed that the level of this sector had been built up 51 centimeters at an earlier time.

The east part of the southeastern wall of this building complex had been built directly against D-Wall-2. It is 0.84 meter thick and, at present, about 2 meters high. The western part of the southeastern wall of the complex is D-Wall-2 itself. Between the southeastern and southwestern walls is a passageway that leads from Sector E to Sector B. The southwestern wall of the

FIG. 17. Building Complex. Sector E.

Fig. 18. Niche in wall of building complex. Sector E.

complex is B-Wall-4; the western, E-Wall-3; the northern, E-Wall-2; and the eastern, E-Wall-1. The latter three walls are the outer walls of the sector which rise above the present ground level about 2 meters. The refined variation of the masonry style is used throughout, and the plaster covering the facing blocks remains in many places.

NICHES

There are four niches in the walls of the units of this building complex (fig. 18). The niches are framed on either side by caliche blocks which are set as posts at right angles to the courses and on top by a third caliche block that rests as a lintel across the other two. The dimensions of the niches vary less than 0.15 meter. They are all approximately 0.45 meter wide and nearly 0.4 meter high and deep. The inside walls are covered with a thin plaster. A test excavation (26A) revealed that one niche is 1 meter above the floor, but the other niches are at varying heights from less than 0.6 meter to more than 1 meter above floor level. Of the three northernmost niches, the westernmost is on the east side of the wall, the center niche on the south side of the wall, and the third on the east side. The fourth niche, to the south, is on the north face of the wall.

PASSAGEWAY

The passageway in the south-central part of the sector leads to Sector B. It is *L*-shaped and extends nearly 12 meters in an east-west direction where it is about 4 meters wide, and nearly 17 meters in a north-south direction where at its widest it is 3.5 meters wide. The south and west walls of the passageway are B-Wall-4, and the north and east walls were built against the ramp or stairway that leads from the ground level of Sector E to the ground level of Sector B, 4.5 meters above. The latter two walls are built in the refined stylistic variation.

OUTER WALLS

E-Wall-1 is nearly 18 meters long, and the eastern border of the sector and part of the eastern border of the main precinct. The bottom 2.5 meters of courses are continuous with the bottom older courses of D-Wall-1. There is, however, a juncture in the upper 2 meters of courses between E-Wall-1 and D-Wall-1. The north end of D-Wall-1 is immediately adjacent to the south end of E-Wall-1, but does not join it. The gap between the two can be measured only in centimeters. E-Wall-1 like D-Wall-1 is 4.5 meters high, but its base is lower than that of D-Wall-1, and so its top is also lower. It is built against the hillslope or built-up side sloping gently inward except for the upper 2 meters which are vertical and form the eastern wall of the building complex. It is not possible to tell from the outside courses where this wall leaves the slope or side and becomes free-standing. The masonry of the lower courses matches the masonry of D-Wall-1 and B-Wall-2; the upper courses, however, have finely made caliche blocks set in even courses.

E-Wall-2 is about 91 meters long and runs from east to west forming the northern border of the sector and the main precinct. It is continuous with E-Wall-1. It was probably more than 6 meters high, and slopes gently inward from base to the ground level of the sector where it becomes vertical. The bottom 4 meters are in the same stylistic variation as B-Wall-2 and D-Wall-1 and the bottom courses of E-Wall-1. The top 2 meters are of the finer masonry of the top courses of E-Wall-1 and the building complexes and Sectors D and E.

APERTURE

There is an aperture in E-Wall-2 which sights on the bank of the Xamilpan River directly below (fig. 19). It was made by leaving a rectangular opening while setting the courses of blocks. On the inside it measures 0.3 meter wide, 0.2 meter high, and 0.4 meter deep. The outside aperture is smaller. It is, at present, at ground level, which means that it was probably less than 0.6 meter above the floor.

E-Wall-3 is on the western border of Sector E, and extends for 21 meters north to south. It is continuous with E-Wall-2. About 4 meters high, its lower courses continue the older lower courses of E-Wall-2 and E-Wall-1, and they are of their stylistic variation. The upper 2 meters appear to have been added later and the masonry is finely made. Much of the plaster remains visible on the upper courses. The lower courses slope inward and the upper courses are vertical. The wall is

FIG. 19. Aperture in E-Wall-2, facing north.

FIG. 20. Gateway, facing northeast. Gatepost is on the left.

built against the hillslope or built-up side and extends more than a meter above the level of the sector.

The juncture between E-Wall-3 and B-Wall-4, which is at right angles to E-Wall-3 no longer exists because the southern portion of E-Wall-3 has broken down completely. It is not possible to determine without excavation the relationship of these two walls.

SECTOR F—OUTSKIRTS OF THE MAIN PRECINCT

OUTER WALL

Along the lower hillslopes of the hill on which the main zone stands are the remnants of walls and other structures. Immediately below C-Wall-1 and B-Wall-6 and paralleling their contours is F-Wall-1 which extends in a northwest-southeast direction for nearly 140 meters. It was built against the hillslope followng its contours, but it is in large part fallen to rubble now. It was probably between 3 and 5 meters high. The facing blocks are roughly made, and the courses are uneven.

DRAINAGE CHANNEL

There is a drainage channel at the eastern end of F-Wall-1. It is about 3 meters long, and extends from the base of the wall to a level area above between F-Wall-1 and B-Wall-6 at an angle of 45°. It is less than 1 meter wide at the base and 2 meters long. The floor and roof of the channel are made of overlapping caliche slabs. The sides are faced in the same way as the outer wall.

GATEPOST (FIG. 20)

Directly opposite the southernmost point of F-Wall-1 to the west is a high post in the shape of a parallel-

epiped. The post is about 2 meters square, and the facing masonry is roughly finished and the courses are uneven.

GATEWAYS TO THE MAIN ZONE (FIG. 20)

There were probably two gateways to the site: one between the gatepost and F-Wall-1, and the second between F-Wall-1 and C-Wall-1. They are now simply open areas with pathways beyond. Perhaps the gates themselves were made of a perishable material.

RECTANGULAR ENCLOSURE

Nine meters north of A-Wall-3 and 9 meters to the west of A-Wall-2 is a rectangular enclosure whose inside measurements are 4.9 meters from north to south and 5.8 feet from east to west with a depth of 0.42 meter. Inside the northwest corner is a stepped platform measuring 3 meters from north to south and 0.67 meter from east to west. The risers are 21 and 24 centimeters high and the tread is 24 centimeters deep. The masonry is standard although there seems to be more rock inclusions in the mortar here than elsewhere. The facing blocks were shaped with some care although without any great precision, and their sizes differ so that even though they are laid in rows, the courses are uneven.

WALLS

A number of low walls were noted on the north hillslope. It is not now possible to follow their extent since many of them have fallen to rubble. The westernmost wall, F-Wall-2, runs north and south at least 10 meters. It is free-standing and about 1 meter high. The facing blocks are fairly well cut, and the courses are even. The wall to the east of it, F-Wall-3, runs parallel to and north of E-Wall-2 and can be followed for 20 meters before it becomes rubble. It is now about 2 meters high, and its facing masonry is the same as F-Wall-2. F-Wall-4 is at right angles to and east of E-Wall-1 and is now about 73 meters long and 2 meters high. Its style is like the latter two walls, and like them it is built against the hillslope. Another small wall, F-Wall-5, is outside the southern border of the main precinct. It measures 2 meters from east to west, and is less than 1 meter high.

These walls may have been built to trap soil being washed down the slope. After several years the accumulated soil provides fertile plots for cultivation.

SUBSITE I

Subsite I is west of the main precinct on a naturally lower level, about 5 meters below the level of the hill on which the main precinct and Subsites II and III stand. That portion of the hill extends for 615 meters in a northeast direction from the main precinct to meet the Xamilpan River at its westernmost point and where it is about 60 meters above the river. The hill is fairly narrow here, and measures little more than 30 meters in some places.

The most striking structure of Subsite I is a mound, about 455 meters to the west of the main precinct. It appears larger than the large mounds of the main precinct. It is now very overgrown, and its present approximate dimensions of 23 meters in diameter and 5 to 6 meters in height are not very meaningful.

About 335 meters to the west of the main precinct and 120 meters to the east of this mound is an arrangement of low walls that are in very poor condition. They are made of roughly shaped caliche blocks that were piled on one another in an irregular pattern, and were once held together by an adobe mortar. Some appear to have been the walls of rooms, and others were set against low hillslopes. The rooms may have constituted the residences of noble families. The architectural stylistic variation here, that is, the use of blocks irregular in size and shape and the lack of regular courses, is similar to that found in C-Wall-2 in the main precinct.

SUBSITE II

Subsite II is directly to the south of the main precinct and is connected to it by a col, that is, a depressed area between the two, measuring 100 meters from north to south and as few as 10 meters from east to west. The subsite is presently cleared because it is used biennially for planting. Its greatest length is 500 meters, north to south. Its width is variable ranging from 23 to 230 meters. There are no structural remains at this subsite, but its surface is densely covered by pottery sherds, and chert and obsidian artifacts which indicate intensive occupation. It is likely that the dwellings were made of perishable material and therefore do not remain.

They probably were like modern peasant dwellings of the Mixteca which are made of pole and thatch. The similarities between modern and prehispanic dwellings in the Mixteca have been described by Cook (1939: pp. 375–385).

SUBSITE III

Subsite III is directly to the east of Subsite II and contiguous with it. It lies about 500 meters southeast of the main precinct. It has been given its own designation because it has structural remains. The main body covers an area of 61 by 72 meters. However, the remnants of walls can be found as many as 30 meters from the main body. The remains consist, primarily, of a quadrangle measuring 55 meters square, and adjoining it on the east is a building complex that can be divided into at least eight units. These may have been the apartments of the nobility. The style of architecture is the same as Subsite I and C-Wall-2 in the main precinct.

SUBSITE IV

This subsite lies on another hill north of the Xamilpan River and about 550 meters northeast of the main precinct. There are the remains of a few structures badly ruined.

SUBSITE V

Subsite V also lies on an adjacent hill about 1,400 meters south of the main precinct. The remains of one structure, badly ruined, were found.

POTTERY

The objectives of the pottery study, determined by the objectives of the investgation as a whole, were to build a chronological framework as a basis for understanding the course of cultural history and the process of cultural change and to specify the cultural affiliations between Tepexi and other sites in order to illuminate its political position.

Since the field work was concerned primarily with mapping, drawing plans of the architecture, and delineating architectural features, excavation was limited. In addition, excavation was not rewarding because outside of the main precinct the hard caliche horizon is less than 30 centimeters from the surface, and there is no accumulative depth. Two test excavations, one in Subsite II and the other in Sector F, were soon abandoned for this reason. In the main precinct, the caliche blocks which had been put down in successive layers to raise the level of the sector were more than 1.5 meters deep in two test pits in Sector A and Sector C. An analysis of the pottery from the mortar between the blocks indicated no chronologically significant distribution. The blocks had been put down at the same time, and the soil of the mortar containing the artifacts apparently had been brought from various places. Another test pit in Sector A revealed disturbed burials with no associated artifacts.

A meter square test pit in Sector E was the only excavation which had both depth and where an unbroken hard caliche horizon was reached (fig. 5). The pottery analysis is based primarily on the material from this pit. The sherds from other pits and from the surface have been used to clarify the classification problems, but have not been used to resolve chronological questions.

The following is a brief description by Dr. Harold E. Malde of the layers based on samples and photographs from the test pit in Sector E.

Layer 1—Sand, non-sorted, stony; light brownish gray (10 YR 6/2, dry); massive (from photo); no conspicuous weathering.

Layer 2—Sand, very fine to fine, non-sorted; light reddish brown (2.5 YR 6/4, dry; 2.5 YR 5/4, moist); hard when dry; includes enough clay to be slightly sticky and slightly plastic when wet; disaggregates in water; effervesces in 1:5 HCl.

Layer 3—Sand, very fine, silty; white (10 YR 8/2, dry; *ca.* 10 YR 7/2, moist); soft when dry; non-sticky and non-plastic when wet; disaggregates in water; effervesces strongly in 1:5 HCl.

Layer 4—Sand, fine to coarse, non-sorted; includes some fine gravel; brown (7.5 YR 5/3, dry); slightly hard when dry; non-sticky when wet but includes enough clay to be slightly plastic; slowly disaggregates in water; effervesces in 1:5 HCl.

Layer 5—Sand, very fine to fine; light gray (10 YR 7/2, dry); consistence when dry indeterminate; non-sticky when wet but very slightly plastic; in part disaggregates readily in water but has some white aggregates (caliche?) that do not disaggregate; effervesces strongly in 1:5 HCl.

Layer 6—Sand, fine to coarse, with some fine gravel; reddish brown (5 YR 5/3 moist, dry color difficult to estimate); many distinct coarse mottles of stronger reddish brown (hue *ca.,* 2.5 YR) visible in photos; slightly hard when dry; disaggregates readily in water (wet color *ca.* 2.5 YR 4/5); slightly sticky but non-plastic when wet; effervesces in 1:5 HCl.

Layer 7—(soil between caliche blocks) Sand, fine to coarse; includes some gravel and subangular aggregates of sandy "soil"; reddish brown (5 YR 4/3– 4/4, moist; *ca.* 5 YR 6/4, dry); porous; slightly hard when dry; non-sticky and non-plastic when wet; disaggregates readily in water; effervesces in 1:5 HCl.

Layer 8—Angular pieces of quartz schist as large as 1 cm., one piece of granite (or fragment from pegmatite), and one piece of freshly broken caliche, in mixture of fine sand and subangular granules of rock (probably also schist); color of sand, brown (*ca.* 7.5 YR 5/3, dry); not aggregated (or disaggregated); slightly plastic when wet; effervesces in 1:5 HCl.

Layer 9—(Charcoal and ash) Charcoal is abundant in pieces as large as 2 cm. Rock fragments of schist and granite (?) are present in angular pieces 0.5 cm. and smaller. One subrounded piece of caliche was found.

Layer 10—Non-sorted mixture of sand and granules of rock and caliche; photo shows scattered angular fragments of rock apparently larger than 10 cm.; under the hand lens shows scattered fragments of charcoal as large as 3 mm.; light brownish gray (10 YR 6/2, dry); slightly hard when dry; very porous; slightly sticky but non-plastic when wet; does not readily disaggregate in water; effervesces in 1:5 HCl.

Layer 11—Resembles Layer 10, but more fragments of caliche are present, and photo shows more angular fragments of rock; dark gray (10 YR 4/1–4/2, dry); wet color much darker, black (10 YR 2/1), which suggests possible presence of finely divided charcoal or other organic material; consistence when dry indeterminate; non-sticky but slightly plastic when wet; effervesces in 1:5 HCl.

The layers do not seem to be the result of natural occurrences, but rather, are cultural strata. They are continuous, that is, there is no important gap in the record when weathering or erosion could have occurred. Thus, we have an indication of a continuous occupation. The first layer is the sandy soil that has been deposited since the construction of the floor. The content of cultural material was of medium density except for the level nearest the floor which had few artifacts. The floor, which has been described above, lies between layer 1 and layer 2. Below the floor are layers 2 to 5 which can be discussed together. Dr. Malde suggests that they "seem to express the residues of at least two efforts at making something from caliche." That is, the white layers 3 and 5 might be powder produced from caliche. Cultural material is sparse throughout. Layer 6 may be either a midden layer or fill brought in from elsewhere, but field observation indicates it is a midden layer. Cultural material is abundant at the bottom levels of this layer. Layer 7 is the caliche construction (described above). It is clear that the soil was brought in from elsewhere to serve as mortar. Layers 8 through 11 may be grouped together. They contain the only conspicuous fragments of schist found in the pit.

Excavation levels were determined by stratification, that is, levels were dug to coincide with layers, except when layers were too thin to make this practicable. Thick layers were divided into convenient arbitrary levels. Excavation proceeded to a depth of 312 cm. where an unbroken hard caliche horizon extended through the area of the test pit and beyond.

Three phases were formulated on the basis of the building construction and the analysis of the pottery. The Huichi phase includes levels 13 through 17. These include layers 8 through 11. The Xaqua phase levels are 5 through 12. These include the layer of caliche construction (layer 7), layer 6 which seems to have been brought in from elsewhere, and layers 5 through 2 which were set down before the construction of the floor. Because the soil in layer 7 and layer 6 was brought in from elsewhere, the pottery in these layers is out of chronological order. It contains both earlier and later types. The earlier types were present as a result of native excavation to obtain soil for these layers. Since at any point in time earlier types are available, but later ones are never obtainable, the later types mark the period. Thus, pottery appearing in both the Huichi phase and Xaqua phase levels is most safely assigned only to the Huichi phase. Pottery found in levels 5 through 12, but not in 13 through 17 are probably of the Xaqua phase. It is not possible to determine from this excavation the continuity of types or modes from the Huichi phase to the Xaqua phase.

The Toyna phase levels are levels 1 through 4. This includes layer 1. Sector E whose architecture is of the refined variety helps define the Toyna phase. The floor of its building complex marks the boundary between the Xaqua and Toyna phases.

Surface collections by a random sampling method were taken from all subsites. Analysis revealed they were all occupied contemporaneously with the main precinct. Their study did not yield a chronological seriation.

The pottery has been classified according to types and modes. The utility of using both these methods in the study of a single collection has been noted by Rouse (1960, 1965; Smith and others, 1960; Sabloff and Smith, 1969). What is most important, however, is that pottery study of Mesoamerica become standardized to permit comparison of collections by means of classificatory systems. Both of these kinds of classification are being used increasingly in the study of collections from Mesoamerican sites, and have been chosen for this study to facilitate future comparisons with the little-studied Mixteca-Puebla region.

The analysis is based on the entire collection of some 5,000 sherds. The preliminary analysis was done at the Instituto Poblano de Antropología e Historia. However, a sufficient representative sample was taken back to the Columbia University laboratory to refine and revise the initial decisions.

In most collections the proportion of decorated sherds and sherds diagnostic of form (such as rim, base, distinctive body sherds, and so on) is smaller than undecorated sherds and sherds with little diagnostic value. In this collection the absence of whole pots and the low absolute number of decorated sherds and sherds diagnostic of form made it difficult to define types and varieties.

It is for this reason that the more generalized "ceramic group" became an important unit in the analysis of the Tepexi collection. It includes sherds which share attributes of paste and surface finish and enough attributes of form and decoration to delineate at least one type-variety and to indicate others. However, the data on form and decoration are insufficient to justify differentiation of the sherds into a number of well-defined types and varieties.

Ware has been used as the most inclusive category. It includes ceramic groups which can be classed together on the basis of paste and surface attributes, but, unlike ceramic groups, are not significant in relation to phases. Since a ware is composed of groups that are *similar* technologically, but shows a *range of variation,* that variation has been expressed by noting the paste and surface attributes of each ceramic group. Thus, groups within the same ware show slightly different expressions of an attribute, such as color, for example. Temper is not considered as an attribute shared by groups within one ware. In this analysis groups with different tempers were placed within one ware.

Because of the lack of whole vessels and the small number of sherds, the number of modes is limited. However, the extrapolation of modes in a small collection does seem to produce a good deal of information on characteristic technology and cultural affiliation, and, thus, for its purposes, was more successful than the use of types which seems to need a larger collection to fulfill its purpose of providing a chronological framework.

Classification is based on the nature of the paste, including features of firing, color, and texture; surface finish; vessel form; and decoration, including motifs and technique. Color designations are derived from Munsell Soil Color Charts. Vessel forms are defined as follows: *bowl*—a vessel with rounded walls, the height of which is less than half, but not less than one-third, the rim diameter; *dish*—a vessel with straight flaring, or outcurving or recurved walls, the height of which varies between one-third and one-fifth of its rim diameter; *plate*—a vessel with straight flaring, out-curviing or recurved walls, the height of which is less than one-fifth of its rim diameter; *jar*—a vessel with a restricted orifice and with a neck separating the rim and the usually rounded body; *griddle*—a plate, generally with straight flaring walls and a flat base with a roughened exterior wall; *incense burner*—the form varies, but for the purposes of this collection, its form is a bowl with an extended handle.

In order to determine in which phase, if any, ceramic groups appeared predominately, a chi-square test was performed. Under the hypothesis that each ceramic group appeared equally (that is, proportionately) in each phase, it would be expected that the number of sherds of each ceramic group in a phase would be proportionate to the total number of sherds in the phase, or in the ratio of the phase sums or approximately 0.15, 0.12, 0.07, 0.66 for the Toyna, Xaqua unmixed, Xaqua mixed, and Huichi, respectively.

The differences between these quantities and the actual number found in phases were used in the chi-square computation. If the distribution were truly proportionate, it would be expected that the chi-square value (with 3 degrees of freedom) would exceed 7.815 only 5 per cent of the time. Therefore, if a chi-square value exceeded 7.815, the hypothesis of equal appearance over the phases was rejected, and it was considered that the ceramic group did predominate in the phase where its presence exceeded the number expected (if proportionate). The decision was generally restricted to those groups whose number of sherds exceeded 68, so that the expected number in each category was at least 5.

Comparisons are based on the literature and on the examination of collections in the Museo Nacional de Antropología (MNA), the Instituto Poblano de Antropología e Historia (IPAH) in Mexico, the American Museum of Natural History (AMNH) in New York, and the Field Museum of Natural History (FMNH) in Chicago.

Tlaltempan Ceramic Group
(fig. 21)

Ware: *Light Red*.

Corpus: 48 sherds.

Paste: Firing: generally fully oxidized. Color: red, light red, and yellowish red (2.5 YR and 5 YR, values 5 and 6, chroma 6 and 8). Temper: rock. Texture: medium to coarse.

Surface: Exterior slipped, interior almost slipped. Finish: matte to lustrous. Color: mostly red (10 R 5/8), though some reddish yellow (5 YR 6/6).

Type-Variety: *Tlaltempan Reddish Brown Painted: Tlaltempan*. Others are indicated.

Form: Vessel form: plate, jar, and bowl. Rim: dish direct, diameter 19 cm.; bowl everted and rolled, diameter 18 cm. Wall thickness: 4–9 mm., most fall within 4–6 mm. range.

Decoration: Painted in dark reddish brown (5 YR 3/2–3). Motif: rim band is common, straight and undulating lines paralleling rim usually in groups of three. Incised line around interior neck of jar and bowl.

Chronological position: Occurs in levels of all 3 phases, but there are too few sherds to judge its chronological position.

Molcaxac Ceramic Group
(fig. 21)

Ware: *Thin Slip Gray-Black*.

Corpus: 16 sherds.

Paste: Firing: some fully oxidized, some incompletely oxidized. Color: light red (2.5 YR 6/8). Temper: rock. Texture: friable, medium.

Surface: Interior and exterior slipped, one interior unslipped. The slip is often thin, and the light-red paste shows through the slip, and in some places the slip does not cover the paste. Finish: in some cases the grooved striations as a result of throwing are prominent. Color: dark gray (5 YR 4/1) over light red (2.5 YR 6/8).

Type-Variety: *Molcaxac Incised:Molcaxac*.

Form: Vessel form: bowl. Rim: direct with tapered lip, slightly everted, and rolled, diameter 18–20 cm. Wall thickness: 3–8 mm.

Decoration: Fine incising. Motif: line paralleling rim, small semi-ovals surrounding spiral.

Chronological position: Occurs in levels of all 3 phases, but there are too few sherds to judge its chronological position.

Comparative material: Itzocan, Tehuacan, and Molcaxac collection in the IPAH. Tehuacan:Teotitlan Incised (Chadwick and MacNeish, 1967).

Almolongo Ceramic Group
(fig. 22)

Ware: *Light Red*.

Corpus: 976 sherds.

Paste: Firing: some fully but most incompletely oxidized. Color: light red (2.5 YR 6/6–8). Temper: coarse to granular rock. Texture: medium to coarse.

Surface: All exteriors and most interiors are slipped. Interiors without slip shown finger impressions. Some interiors are scraped and slipped. Finish: exteriors are polished, some to a dull-lustrous finish, but most are matte. Color: red to light red (2.5 YR 4/8–6/8).

Type-Variety: *Almolongo Red:Almolongo*. Others are indicated.

Form: Vessel form: jar, bowl, and griddle. Rim: jar sharply everted, diameter 14–28 cm.; bowl direct or slightly everted, diameter 24–32 cm.; griddle direct, ridged with tapered lip. Appendage: strap handle. Support: conical, 17 mm. is widest diameter. Base: flat and annular. Vessel floor: bowl deeply incised with parallel lines 6 mm. apart and between these are deeply incised crescents 4 mm. apart.

Decoration: None.

Chronological position: Occurs in levels of all 3 phases, but is predominately in the Huichi phase.

Chochos Ceramic Group
(fig. 22)

Ware: *Reddish Unslipped*.

Corpus: 457 sherds.

Paste: Firing: most are fully oxidized, only a few are incompletely oxidized. Color: red (10 R 5/8). Temper: quartz; heavily tempered; coarse to granular. Texture: medium to coarse, highly friable.

Surface: Unslipped, smoothed interior, some smoothed interior and exterior, and some interiors scraped leaving pits and uneven surface. Color: same as paste.

FIG. 21. Top row: Molcaxac Incised, Comulco Gray, Canal Black, Mila Incised. 2nd row: El Zapote Molded, Mimiapan Black, Xolochta Finely Incised, Coixtlahuaca Black. 3rd row: Tepexi Brown Painted, Tepexi Brown Painted, Tepeaca Red Painted. 4th row: Tepexi Group, Zacapala Dark Brown Painted, Ayutla Red/Gray. Bottom row: Tlaltempan Reddish Brown Painted, Xamilpan Pink/Brown, Balsas Red Painted, Zacapala Dark Brown Painted. Scale 1:2.5

Type-Variety: *Chochos Red: Chochos.* Others are indicated.

Form: Vessel form: dish and griddle. Rim: dish direct; griddle direct, ridged, with tapered lip. Wall thickness: 4–14 mm. (extremes).

Decoration: None.

Chronological position: Occurs in levels of all 3 phases, but is predominately in the Huichi phase.

Huajoyuca Ceramic Group
(fig. 22)

Ware: *Red-Yellow.*
Corpus: 1028 sherds.

Paste: Firing: some fully, but most incompletely oxidized. Color: reddish yellow and yellowish red (5 YR 5/8–6/8). Temper: rock. Texture: fine.

Surface: Slipped interior and exterior. Finish: dull-lustrous to matte. Color: yellowish red and reddish yellow (5 YR 5/8–7/8), some reddish brown (5 YR 4/3–4/8).

Type-Variety: *Huajoyuca Reddish Yellow: Huajoyuca.* Others are indicated.

Form: Vessel form: bowl, jar, and griddle. Rim: bowl direct or slightly everted, diameter is 18 cm.; jar strongly everted, diameter 28 cm., griddle direct,

FIG. 22.   Top row: Acatlan Polychrome, Mixtec Polychrome, Cholula Polychrome.   2nd row: Ocotlan Graphite, Rosario Black/ Red, Gracias White Painted.   3rd row: Calco Light Red, Huajoyuca Reddish Yellow, Ixcaquistla Speckled.   4th row: Huajuapan Domestic Thin Orange, Hondo Grayish Brown, Chochos Red, Yagul Gray.   Bottom row: Almolongo Red, Cuautempam Silvery, Xochitlan Chalky Slip, Coatepetl Reddish Brown.   Scale 1:2.5

marked ridged rim with tapered lip. Appendage: jar strap handle, 4 cm. long or less; nubbin lug.

Decoration: None.

Chronological position: Occurs in levels of all 3 phases, but is predominately in the Huichi phase.

Tepexi Ceramic Group
(fig. 21)

Ware: *Red-Yellow.*

Corpus: 150 sherds.

Paste: Firing: generally fully oxidized, some are partially oxidized. Color: yellowish red to reddish yellow (5 YR 5/8–6/8). Temper: unidentified white particles of medium size. Texture: fine.

Surface: Slipped interior and exterior. Finish: highly lustrous to matte. Color: yellowish red to reddish yellow (5 YR 5/6–8 to 6/6–8); some gray (5 YR 6/1–2).

Type-Variety: *Tepexi Brown Painted:Tepexi.* Others are indicated.

Form: Vessel form: bowl, plate, and jar. Rim: bowl direct with tapered lip, diameter is 12 cm.; plate direct with tapered lip, diameter is 13 cm.; jar everted, diameter is 24 cm. Base: bowl rounded, obtuse angle with slightly convex interior. Appendage: jar nubbin lug. Vessel height: bowl 48 mm.; plate 25 mm. Wall thickness: bowl 5–7 mm.; plate 2–4 mm.; jar 6–8 mm.

Decoration: Painted in reddish brown and dark reddish brown (5 YR 4/3, 3/3–4). Bowl and plate have decoration on the interior only. Jar has occasional interior rim band, otherwise decoration is on exterior. Motif: rim band, undulating and straight lines paralleling rim, fret, and spiral.

Chronological position: Occurs in levels of all 3 phases, but is predominately in the Huichi phase.

Comparative material: Tepeaca, Huehuetlan, Molcaxac, Chiquihuite, and San Francisco de Asis Tetla (Totimehuacan) collection in the IPAH. Yanhuitlan and Nochistlan collections in AMNH.

Yagul Ceramic Group
(fig. 22)

Ware: *Fine Gray.*

Corpus: 25 sherds.

Paste: Firing: unoxidized or reduced. Color: light gray (10 YR 7/1). Temper: unidentified white particles. Texture: very fine.

Surface: Exterior slipped, interior not slipped (one sherd has interior slipped.) Finish: exterior has medium luster, interior is smooth and compact. Color: gray (5 YR 6/1).

Type-Variety: *Yagul Gray:Yagul.*

Form: Vessel form: bowl. Rim: direct with tapered lip, diameter 15 cm. Wall thickness: 4 mm.

Decoration: None.

Chronological position: Occurs in the Huichi phase exclusively, but there are too few sherds for the chi-square test to be applicable.

Comparative material: Coixtlahuaca (Bernal, 1948–1949: pp. 41–42), Yagul: fine gray ware (*Meso-american Notes,* 1955: p. 74).

Mila Ceramic Group
(fig. 21)

Ware: Unspecified.

Corpus: 10 sherds.

Paste: Firing: fully oxidized. Color: light reddish brown (5 YR 6/4). Temper: rock. Texture: medium.

Surface: Exterior is always slipped, interior is sometimes slipped, sometimes unslipped and smooth and compact. Finish: thick slip and slipped surface is generally lustrous. Color: dark reddish gray (10 R 3/1), one sherd of red, (2.4 YR 5/6).

Type-Variety: *Mila Incised:Mila.*

Form: Vessel form: insufficient data. Rim: direct and rolled, diameter 18 cm. Wall thickness: 6–8 mm.

Decoration: Groove incising. Motif: undulating line perhaps representing snake, vertical lines, V's, zigzags; motifs are placed between lines paralleling rim which form a band.

Chronological position: Occurs in Huichi levels exclusively, but there are too few sherds for the chi-square test to be applicable.

Comparative material: Tehuacan collection at the IPAH, Tehuacan: Teotitlan Incised (Chadwick and MacNeish, 1967).

Zacapala Ceramic Group
(fig. 21)

Ware: *Red-Yellow.*

Corpus: 8 sherds.

Paste: Firing: fully oxidized. Color: light red (2.5 YR 6/6–8). Temper: unidentified white particles. Texture: very fine to silty.

Surface: Exterior and interior slipped. Finish: exterior slip is thin and dull-lustrous, interior slip is thicker and highly lustrous. Color: exterior is light red (2.5 YR 6/8), interior is reddish yellow (5 YR 6/6).

Type-Variety: *Zacapala Dark Brown Painted:Zacapala.*

Form: Vessel form: possibly bowl and dish. Rim: everted, rolled. Support: triangular with lateral perforation, length 7 cm., width 3 cm. tapering to 1 cm. Wall thickness: 6 mm.

Decoration: Painted in dark brown (7.5 YR 3/4–4/4). Motif: spiral, interior rim band, straight and undulating lines paralleling rim, short and long vertical lines.

Chronological position: Occurs in Huichi levels exclusively, but there are too few sherds for the chi-square test to be applicable.

Comparative material: Tepozuchil and San Francisco de Asis Tetla (Totimehuacan) collection in the IPAH and Zautla vessel in FMNH.

Xochitlan Ceramic Group
(fig. 22)

Ware: Unspecified.

Corpus: 4 sherds.

Paste: Firing: fully oxidized and smudged. Color: light reddish brown (5 YR 6/4) and very dark gray (5 YR 3/1). Temper: mica is predominate ranging from medium to pebble size. Texture: fine to medium.

Surface: Slipped interior and exterior with a chalky slip. Finish: matte. Color: pinkish white-pinkish gray (7.5 YR 8/2–7/2).

Type-Variety: *Xochitlan Chalky Slip:Xochitlan.*

Form: Vessel form: probably jar. Rim: slightly everted, diameter 10 cm. Appendage: strap handle, width 2 cm., length 7 cm. Wall thickness: 5–7 mm.

Decoration: None.

Chronological position: Occurs in Huichi levels exclusively, but there are too few sherds for the chi-square test to be applicable.

Gracias Ceramic Group
(fig. 22)

Ware: *Lustrous Red.*

Corpus: 6 sherds.

Paste: Firing: incompletely oxidized. Color: brown (7.5 YR 5/4). Temper: rock. Texture: medium.

Surface: Exterior and interior slipped. Finish: highly lustrous interior and exterior rim, otherwise matte. Color: red (10 R 4/6) is exterior and interior rim color: the exterior body shades into higher values.

Type-Variety: *Gracias White Painted:Gracias.*

Form: Vessel form: possibly bowl. Rim: direct and inverted, diameter 15 cm. Wall thickness: 6–8 mm.

Decoration: Painted white (5 YR 8/1) and incised. Motif: incised designs (fragmentary) filled in with white.

Chronological position: Occurs in Huichi levels exclusively, but there are too few sherds for the chi-square test to be applicable.

Comparative material: Valley of Mexico: Red Ware (Tolstoy, 1958: pp. 45–47).

El Zapote Ceramic Group
(fig. 21)

Ware: *Reddish Brown.*

Corpus: 20 sherds.

Paste: Firing: most are incompletely oxidized. Color: red to light red (2.5 YR 5/8–6/8). Temper: sparsely tempered with quartz. Texture: medium.

Surface: Interior and exterior are slipped. Finish: medium-lustrous to matte. Color: red, light red, light reddish brown (2.5 YR 5/8, 6/6, 6/4).

Type-Variety: *El Zapote Molded:El Zapote.*

Form: Vessel form: insufficient data. Rim: direct with tapered lip. Support: conical with lateral perforations. Wall thickness: 5–10 mm.

Decoration: Molded. Raised nodes, crescents, undulating lines, parallel lines and chevrons, floor of vessel and lower inner walls are decorated.

Chronological position: Occurs in Huichi and Xaqua levels, but there are too few sherds for the chi-square test to be applicable. However, it may be Huichi phase predominately.

Comparative material: Similar to Acatlan Polychrome (see below). The decorative motifs and the position of the decoration on the vessel are the same. Perhaps the same molds were used with different paste. Chiquihuite, Tepozuchil, and Molcaxac collections in the IPAH.

Tepeaca Ceramic Group
(fig. 21)

Ware: *Red-Yellow.*

Corpus: 40 sherds.

Paste: Firing: generally fully oxidized. Color: light red to reddish brown (2.5 YR 6/8, 5 YR 5/4). Temper: unidentified white particles. Texture: very fine to silty.

Surface: Slipped interior and exterior. Color: light reddish brown to reddish yellow (5 YR 6/4–6). Finish: matte.

Type-Variety: *Tepeaca Red Painted:Tepeaca.* Others are indicated.

Form: Vessel form: bowl and dish. Rim: direct with tapered lip, bowl diameter 11 cm., dish diameter 20 cm. Base: round obtuse angle. Wall thickness: 3–5 mm. Height: bowl 5 cm.

Decoration: Painted interior and exterior in red (7.5 R 3/4–4/4) and very dusky red (2.5 YR 2/2). Motif: rim band (5–9 mm. wide), straight lines parallel to rim, and undulating lines diagonal to rim. Bowls: motifs on exterior except for rim band. Dish: motifs on interior only.

Chronological position: Occurs in Huichi and Xaqua levels, but there are too few sherds to judge its chronological position.

Comparative material: Tepeaca (Noguera, 1954: p. 235, no. 4), Tehuacan, Tepeaca, and Huehuetlan collections at the IPAH, and the Yanhuitlan collection at the AMNH. Mixteca Alta: Red on Cream (MNA).

Ocotlan Ceramic Group
(fig. 22)

Ware: *Lustrous Red.*

Corpus: 5 sherds.

Paste: Firing: incompletely oxidized. Color: reddish brown (5 YR 5/4). Temper: unidentified white particles. Texture: medium.

Surface: Slipped interior and exterior. Finish: medium lustrous. Color: red (7.5 R 4/6).

Type-Variety: *Ocotlan Graphite:Ocotlan.*

Form: Vessel form: bowl. Rim: direct, with tapered lip, diameter 14 cm. Wall thickness: 6–7 mm.

Decoration: Thick, very dark gray (7.5 R N3/0) band of graphite paralleling the rim.

Chronological position: Occurs in Huichi and Xaqua levels, but there are too few sherds to judge its chronological position.

Comparative material: Coixtlahuaca, Yagul: Mixtec graphite on red (*Mesoamerican Notes* 1955: p. 39, fig. 21), Zaachila: graphite on red-orange (Bernal, 1966a: p. 355).

Cuautempam Ceramic Group
(fig. 22)

Ware: *Reddish Unslipped.*

Corpus: 30 sherds.

Paste: Firing: generally incompletely oxidized, some smudged. Color: red (10 R 5/6). Temper: some quartz, but mica predominates; mica particles are fine to coarse; heavily tempered. Texture: medium.

Surface: Unslipped, smoothed. Color: same as paste, but speckled with gray and silver because of the numerous mica particles of various sizes.

Type-Variety: *Cuautempam Silvery:Cuautempam.* Others are indicated.

Form: Vessel form: jar. Rim: everted and direct, both with tapered lip, diameter 20 cm. Wall thickness: 6–8 mm.

Decoration: None.

Chronological position: Occurs in levels of all 3 phases, but there are too few sherds for the chi-square test to be applicable. However, it may be predominately in the Xaqua phase.

Calco Ceramic Group
(fig. 22)

Ware: *Reddish Unslipped.*

Corpus: 410 sherds.

Paste: Firing: almost all are incompletely oxidized. Color: light red (10 R 6/4). Temper: rock. Texture: medium to coarse, laminated, friable.

Surface: Unslipped, scraped. Color: same as paste.

Type-Variety: *Calco Light Red:Calco.* Others are indicated.

Form: Vessel form: jar and griddle. Rim: jar everted with tapered lip, diameter is 22 cm.; griddle direct, ridged with tapered lip. Appendages: jar strap handle at right angles to rim, length 7 cm., width 3–5 cm. Wall thickness: jar and griddle about 1 cm.

Decoration: None.

Chronological position: Occurs in levels of all 3 phases, but is predominately in the Xaqua phase.

Hondo Ceramic Group
(fig. 22)

Ware: *Grayish Brown.*

Corpus: 195 sherds.

Paste: Firing: fully and incompletely oxidized. Color: dark reddish gray to light brown (5 YR 4/2 and 5 and 6 values and 3, 4, and 6 chromas). Temper: unidentified fine white particles. Texture: very fine to silty.

Surface: Slipped exterior and interior. The dark grayish brown slip is applied unevenly and the lighter color shows through here and there. Finish: notably smooth and compact, dull-lustrous to matte. Color: same as paste and dark grayish brown (10 YR 4/2).

Type-Variety: *Hondo Grayish Brown:Hondo.* Others are indicated.

Form: Vessel form: plate, bowl, and griddle. Base: plate slightly concave. Wall thickness: 5–6 mm.

Decoration: None.

Chronological position: Occurs in levels of all 3 phases, but is predominately in the Xaqua phase.

Canal Ceramic Group
(fig. 21)

Ware: Unspecified.

Corpus: 180 sherds.

Paste: Firing: fully oxidized. Color: light reddish brown (5 YR 6/3). Temper: rock. Texture: fine.

Surface: Interior and exterior slipped. Finish: lustrous. Color: black (2.5 YR N2/0).

Type-Variety: *Canal Black:Canal.* Others are indicated.

Form: Vessel form: jar. Rim: slightly and sharply everted, both with tapered lip, diameter 20 cm. Wall thickness: 6–7 mm.

Decoration: None.

Chronological position: Occurs in levels of all 3 phases, but is predominately in the Xaqua phase.

Comulco Ceramic Group
(fig. 21)

Ware: *Thin Slip Gray-Black.*

Corpus: 101 sherds.

Paste: Firing: some fully oxidized, some incompletely oxidized. Color: light red (2.5 YR 6/8). Temper: rock. Texture: medium.

Surface: Exterior slipped, interiors generally unslipped, except for griddle where interior is always slipped, exterior unslipped. Finish: slip is thin, and light red paste shows through the slip; slipped surface generally matte, although some have slight luster; unslipped surface smooth and compact except for griddle which is scraped. Color: dark gray (5 YR 4/1) and very dark gray (2.5 YR 3/0).

Type-Variety: *Comulco Gray: Comulco.* Others are indicated.

Form. Vessel form: bowl, griddle and jar. Rim: bowl everted, thickened; griddle everted, ridged with tapered lip; jar everted with tapered lip, diameter 14 cm. Wall thickness: bowl 6 mm.; griddle 9 mm.; jar 6 mm.

Decoration: None.

Chronological position: Occurs in levels of all 3 phases, but is predominately in the Xaqua phase.

Comparative material: Itzocan and Huehuetlan collections at the IPAH.

Mimiapan Ceramic Group
(fig. 21)

Ware: Unspecified.

Corpus: 149 sherds.

Paste: Firing: incompletely or fully oxidized. Color: dark reddish brown (5 YR 3/3). Temper: mica predominates. Texture: medium.

Surface: Thin slip which wears away easily. Slip on exterior only. Finish: matte. Color: black (2.5 YR N2/0).

Type-Variety: *Mimiapan Black:Mimiapan.*

Form: Vessel form: bowl and griddle. Rim: bowl inverted with slightly tapered lip, diameter 14 cm. Wall thickness: bowl 2–3 mm., griddle 6 mm.

Decoration: None.

Chronological position: Occurs in Huichi and Xaqua levels, but is predominately in the Xaqua phase.

Ayutla Ceramic Group
(fig. 21)

Ware: Unspecified.

Corpus: 5 sherds.

Paste: Firing: fully or incompletely oxidized. Color: brown (7.5 YR 5/2). Temper: sand and rock; heavily tempered. Texture: medium to coarse, highly friable.

Surface: Slipped interior and exterior. Slip is thin. Finish: dull-lustrous. Color: dark gray (10 YR 4/1).

Type-Variety: *Ayutla Red/Gray:Ayutla.*

Form: Vessel form: insufficient data. Rim: slightly everted with tapered lip, diameter 18 cm. Wall thickness: 6–7 mm.

Decoration: Painted red (7.5 YR 5/8) lip band.

Chronological position: Occurs in Xaqua levels exclusively, but there are too few sherds for the chi-square test to be applicable.

Coixtlahuaca Ceramic Group
(fig. 21)

Ware: Unspecified.

Corpus: 10 sherds.

Paste: Firing: partially oxidized. Color: pinkish gray (5 YR 6/2). Temper: does not appear tempered. Texture: silty to very fine.

Surface: Slipped interior and exterior. Finish: medium luster. Color: very dark gray to black (2.5 YR N3/0, N2/0).

Type-Variety: *Coixtlahuaca Black:Coixtlahuaca.*

Form: Vessel form: insufficient data. Rim: slightly everted with tapered lip, diameter 18 cm. Wall thickness: 4 mm.

Decoration: None.

Chronological position: Occurs in a Xaqua level exclusively, but there are too few sherds for the chi-square test to be applicable.

Xamilpan Ceramic Group
(fig. 21)

Ware: Unspecified.

Corpus: 10 sherds.

Paste: Firing: unoxidized or reduced, some partially oxidized. Color: pinkish gray to pink (7.5 YR 7/2–4). Temper: rock. Texture: coarse.

Surface: Slipped interior and exterior. Surface is uneven. Particles are felt on surface through the slip. Color: light brown (7.5 YR 6/4).

Type-Variety: *Xamilpan Pink/Brown:Xamilpan.*

Form: Vessel form: dish and/or bowl. Rim: direct with tapered lip. Support: slab, crenelated and slanted. Wall thickness: 4–5 mm.

Decoration: Painted in dusky red (7.5 R 3/2) unevenly. Motif: bands at bottom of support, exterior and interior, and on lip, and on interior rim.

Chronological position: Occurs in levels of the Xaqua phase exclusively, but there are too few sherds for the chi-square test to be applicable.

Balsas Ceramic Group
(fig. 21)

Ware: *Fine Gray.*

Corpus: 11 sherds.

Paste: Firing: unoxidized or smudged, may be reduced. Color: dark gray (2.5 YR N4/0). Temper: unidentified fine white particles. Texture: silty to very fine, laminated.

Surface: Slipped interior and exterior. Finish: matte. Color: pink (7.5 YR 7/4) and gray (10 YR 6/1).

Type-Variety: *Balsas Red Painted:Balsas.*

Form: Vessel form: plate, height 3 cm. Rim: direct, diameter 22 cm. Support: straight slab. Wall thickness: 4–6 mm.

Decoration: Painted in dusky and weak red (7.5 YR 3/4–4/4). Negative and positive painting technique used. Both interior and exterior of body and interior and exterior of rim were painted. Motif: spiral, step-fret, paired parallel vertical lines, and straight line paralleling rim.

Chronological position: Occurs in Toyna phase levels exclusively, but there are too few sherds for the chi-square test to be applicable.

Rosario Ceramic Group
(fig. 22)

Ware: *Lustrous Red.*

Corpus: 4 sherds.

Paste: Firing: generally incompletely oxidized. Color: brown (7.5 YR 5/4). Temper: rock. Texture: medium.

Surface: Entire exterior and interior rim is slipped. The rest of the interior is unslipped. Finish: slipped surface is highly lustrous. Color: weak red (10 R 4/4).

Type-Variety: *Rosario Black/Red:Rosario.*

Decoration: Painted black (7.5 R N2/0) line around neck.

Chronological position: Occurs in Toyna phase levels only, but there are too few sherds for the chi-square test to be applicable.

Comparative material: Valley of Mexico:Red Ware (Tolstoy, 1958: pp. 45–47).

Xolochta Ceramic Group
(fig. 21)

Ware: Unspecified.

Corpus: 34 sherds.

Paste: Firing: some unoxidized or reduced and some appear smudged. Color: gray (7.5 R N5/0) to black (7.5 R N2/0). Temper: does not appear tempered. Texture: silty.

Surface: Slipped exterior, unslipped interior. Finish: exterior-matte to medium lustrous, interior-smoothed. Color: dark gray to black (7.5 YR N4/0–N2/0).

Type-Variety: *Xolochta Finely Incised:Xolochta.*

Form: Vessel form: insufficient data. Appendages: hollowed cylindrical handle, length 5 cm., width 4.7 cm., height 2.4 cm. Wall thickness: 4–5 mm.

Decoration: Fine incising. Motif: stepped undulating line which may represent a snake, spiral.

Chronological position: Occurs in Toyna phase levels exclusively, but there are too few sherds for the chi-square test to be applicable.

Coatepetl Ceramic Group
(fig. 22)

Ware: *Reddish Brown.*

Corpus: 664 sherds.

Paste: Firing: some fully, most incompletely, oxidized. Color: reddish brown (2.5 YR 5/4). Temper: rock. Texture: medium

Surface: Thin slip, exterior and interior. Finish: matte. Color: reddish brown to weak red (2.5 YR 5/4–2).

Type-Variety: *Coatepetl Reddish Brown:Coatepetl.* Others are indicated.

Form: Vessel form: jar, bowl, griddle, and plate. Rim: jar everted with slightly tapered lip, diameter 34 cm.; bowl direct, thickened and slightly inverted with tapered lip, diameter 34 cm. Wall thickness: all forms 4–6 mm. Appendage: jar strap handle, width 2.5 cm., length 2.5 cm. Support: bifurcate nubbin, length 3.3 cm., width 2 cm.

Decoration: None.

Chronological position: Occurs in levels of all 3 phases, but is predominately in the Toyna phase.

Ixcaquistla Ceramic Group
(fig. 22)

Ware: *Light Red.*

Corpus: 138 sherds.

Paste: Firing: generally incompletely oxidized. Color: red (2.5 YR 5/6–8). Temper: quartz and mica, mica predominates, particles are coarse to granular, heavily tempered. Texture: medium.

Surface: Slipped exterior, unslipped and slipped interior. Finish: dull-lustrous. Color: red to light red (2.5 YR 5/8–6/6), but appears speckled with gray because of the numerous mica particles.

Type-Variety: *Ixcaquistla Speckled:Ixcaquistla.*

Form: Vessel form: griddle, jar, and possibly incense burner. Rim: griddle, direct, ridged, diameter 40 cm.; jar sharply everted, diameter 14 cm. and direct with tapered lip and faint groove, diameter 24 cm. Appendage: incense burner, flattened cylindrical handle, diameter 16 cm. Wall thickness: 3–6 mm.

Decoration: None.

Chronological position: Occurs in the Toyna phase exclusively, and the chi-square test places it predominately in the Toyna phase.

Comparative material: Ixcaquistla (Landa Abrego, 1966: personal communication).

SPECIAL TYPES

Huajuapan Domestic Thin Orange
(fig. 22)

Corpus: 13 sherds.

Paste: Firing: fully oxidized, but some incompletely oxidized. Color: yellowish red (5 YR 5/8) and reddish yellow (5 YR 6/8 and 7 YR 7/6). Temper: unidentified. Texture: medium grainy.

Surface: Appears unslipped and polished. Finish: matte. Color: as above.

Form: Vessel form: insufficient data, possibly bowl. Rim: slightly inverted, thickened, diameter 8 cm.

Decoration: None.

Chronological position: Appears in Huichi phase levels only, but number of sherds is too small for the chi-square test to be applicable.

Comparative material: Paddock (1966: pp. 176–182) suggests that imitations of Thin Orange pottery were made in southern Puebla during the Ñuiñe period.

Mixtec Polychrome
(fig. 22)

Corpus: 6 sherds.

Paste: Firing: fully oxidized. Color: red (2.5 YR 5/6). Temper: unidentified. Texture: very fine.

Surface: Interior and exterior slipped. Finish: highly lustrous.

Form: Vessel form: bowl. Rim: slightly everted, thickened, diameter 10 cm., height 4 cm. Wall thickness: 3 mm.

Decoration: Painted in pink (5 YR 8/3), red (5 R 4/8), dusky red (5 R 3/4), reddish black (5 R 2/1), and light red (10 R 6/8) on exterior and interior. Motif: spiral and step in combination, short parallel vertical lines, circles and repetitive lines. Motifs cover the entire field in an interlocking pattern.

Chronological position: Occurs in Huichi phase levels, but number is too small for the chi-square test to be applicable.

Comparative material: This is one of the types of Mixtec Polychrome and shares many decorative attributes with Cholula Polychrome (see Paddock 1966: pp. 201, 207, 209, 227, 301, 337–343, plates 18–40). Mixtec Polychrome types have not yet been classified.

Acatlan Polychrome
(fig. 22)

Corpus: 33 sherds.

Paste: Firing: fully and incompletely oxidized and partially oxidized. Color: light reddish brown to red (2.5 YR 6/4, 5/8). Temper: unidentified white particles. Texture: fine to medium.

Surface: Slipped interior and exterior. Finish: medium lustrous. Color: light brown (7.5 YR 6/4) and light red (2.5 YR 6/8) are extremes, most are reddish yellow (5 YR 6/6, 7/6).

Form: Vessel form: bowl and possibly dish. Rim: sharply everted with tapered lip. Dimensions: bowl diameter 13–14 cm., height 4–6 cm. Wall thickness: 4–6 mm. Support: straight slab, slanted crenelated slab.

Decoration: Painted in red (7.5 R 4/6), dusky red (7.5 R 3/2), black (7.5 R N2/0) and white 5 YR 8/1). Motif: cross-cutting parallel lines with dot in squares so formed, spiral with step, circles, diagonal parallel lines. Molded design on vessel floor and lower inner walls. Motif: nodes, parallel lines.

Chronological position: Appears in Huichi and Xaqua phase levels but number is too small to judge its chronological position.

Comparative material: Cuicatlan, Jayacatlan, Tehuantepec, Coixtlahuaca, Santa Maria Ixcatlan, Acatlan, Calipan, Cholula, Culhuacan (Espejo, 1949: p. 103; Noguera, 1940: lam. 16–18; Seler-Sachs, 1949, Franco, 1955; Foster, 1960; Moser, 1969).

Various Unclassified Polychromes

Corpus: 39.

Many of these sherds have the motif elements found in the Mixtec and Cholula Polychromes. Others have the characteristics of Acatlan Polychrome, that is, there is a buff color base with dusky red, black, and white paint with some negative painting. Others resemble Veracruz types especially in the attribute of a polished and highly lustrous white ground as well as elements of design. Possible types are represented by one or at most three sherds, and because of the complexity of color and decoration as well as the lack of information on form, it is not possible to classify or describe the attributes which constitute a defined type or a ceramic group.

Wares and Types described Elsewhere in Detail
(fig. 22)

Cholula Polychrome Noguera, 1954: pp. 120–154. Cholulteca I, II, and III.

Chronological position at Tepexi: Occurs in levels of all 3 phases, but is predominately in the Toyna phase.

Plumbate: Shepard, 1948. Tula period.

Chronological position at Tepexi: Occurs in Huichi and Xaqua phase levels in a small number.

Texcoco Moulded: Tolstoy, 1958: pp. 35, 49, 50, 63. Occurs in the Late Aztec (Post-B), but probably begins slightly before time B.

Chronological position at Tepexi: Occurs in the Huichi phase levels only in a small number.

Culhuacan Black/Orange: Tolstoy, 1958: pp. 35, 47, 48, 62, 69. Tula period (Pre-C) and Early Aztec (C-B). Griffin and Espejo 1950; Franco, 1949 (Aztec I–II).

Chronological position at Tepexi: Occurs in Huichi and Xaqua phase levels, but is predominately in the Huichi phase.

Tenochtitlan Black/Orange: Tolstoy, 1958: pp. 8, 14, 35, 46, 47, 48, 61, 63. Occurs in Early Aztec (C-B), but its peak is reached in Late Aztec (Post-B). Griffin and Espejo, 1950; Franco, 1949 (Aztec II–III).

Chronological position at Tepexi: Occurs exclusively in the Huichi phase in a small number.

Tlatelolco Black/Orange: Tolstoy, 1958: pp. 35, 47 48, 63, 64. Occurs in Late Aztec (Post B), but in western part of the Valley of Mexico it occurs around Time A only. Griffin and Espejo, 1950; Franco, 1949 (Aztec IV).

Chronological position at Tepexi: Occurs in a small number in the Toyna phase only.

Texcoco Black and White/Red: Tolstoy, 1958: pp. 35, 45, 46, 47, 63, 64, 69. Appears most frequently in Early Aztec (C-B), also appears in Late Aztec (Post-B) as well.

Chronological position at Tepexi: Occurs in levels of all 3 phases in a small number.

Texcoco Black/Red: Tolstoy, 1958: pp. 35, 45, 46, 47, 61, 63, 64. Occurs in Early Aztec (C-B), but appears most frequently in Late Aztec (Post-B).

Chronological position at Tepexi: Occurs in levels of all 3 phases in a small number.

Texcoco Black/Red Incised: Tolstoy, 1958: pp. 47, 63, 69. Appears in Early Aztec (C-B).

Chronological position at Tepexi: Occurs in levels of all 3 phases in a small number.

The following modes provide an indication of Tepexi's relation with the Mixteca-Puebla region as well as with other regions of Mesoamerica, and some information on technological and artistic procedures.

Present in All Phases

Straight slab support: Acatlan Polychrome, Balsas Red Painted:Balsas.

Comparative material: Cuicatlan, Jayacatlan, Coixtlahuaca, Santa Maria Ixcatlan, Acatlan, Calipan, Culhuacan (Seler-Sachs, 1949; Espejo, 1949); Valley of Mexico (Tolstoy, 1958: fig. 3, pp. 32, 34, 58, 67).

Painted dotted circle motif: Mixtec Polychrome, Acatlan Polychrome, Cholula Polychrome.

Comparative material: Mixtec collection (sites unidentified) in the MNA, Cuicatlan, Jayacatlan, Coixtlahuaca, Santa Maria Ixcatlan, Acatlan, Calipan, Culhuacan (Seler-Sachs, 1949; Espejo, 1949);

Zaachila (Paddock, 1966: pls. 20–22); Cholula (Noguera, 1954).

Painting in more than three colors: Mixtec Polychrome, Cholula Polychrome, Acatlan Polychrome.

Comparative material: Mixtec collection (sites unidentified) in the MNA. Zaachila and Yagul (Paddock, 1966: pls. 18–39), Cholula (Noguera, 1954), Monte Albán V (Caso and Acosta, 1967), Coixtlahuaca (Bernal, 1948–49).

Decorative field entirely covered with motifs in an interlocking pattern: Mixtec Polychrome, Cholula Polychrome.

Comparative material: Mixtec collection (sites unidentified) in the MNA, Zaachila (Paddock, 1966: pls. 25–27, 29), Cholula (Noguera, 1954), Monte Albán V (Caso and Acosta, 1967).

Painted spiral and step motif in combination: Mixtec Polychrome, Cholula Polychrome, Acatlan Polychrome.

Comparative material: Mixtec collections (sites unidentified) in the MNA, Zaachila, and Yagul (Paddock, 1966: pls. 27, 32, 33, 35) Cholula (Noguera, 1954).

Thin gray-black slip: Molcaxac Incised:Molcaxac. Comulco Gray:Comulco, Mimiapan Black:Mimiapan.

Comparative material: Itzocan, Tehuacan collections in the IPAH.

Decorative motifs resembling elements in the Codex Borgia: Molcaxac Incised:Molcaxac, Mila Incised: Mila, Xolochta Finely Incised:Xolochta, Tepexi

TABLE 1

NUMBER OF SHERDS IN EACH LEVEL

LEVELS	TOYNA PHASE				XAQUA PHASE UNMIXED				XAQUA PHASE MIXED				HUICHI PHASE					OTHER LOCATIONS	TOTAL
	1	2	3	4	5	6	7	8	9	10	11	12	13	14	15	16	17		
TLALTEMPAN	1	0	1	1	0	0	1	2	2	1	1	2	0	2	11	3	0	20	48
MOLCAXAC	0	0	0	1	0	1	0	1	2	0	0	0	0	1	2	0	0	8	16
ALMOLONGO	13	21	15	15	12	1	16	47	22	14	8	6	24	84	201	169	102	206	976
CHOCHOS	11	27	21	5	5	4	5	0	5	5	2	1	12	26	44	67	203	14	457
HUAJOYUCA	10	0	7	6	11	1	6	22	5	17	16	9	28	67	87	91	77	568	1028
TEPEXI	0	0	0	1	2	0	3	8	2	2	0	0	7	28	38	1	0	58	150
YAGUL	0	0	0	0	0	0	0	0	0	0	0	0	0	0	16	0	2	7	25
MILA	0	0	0	0	0	0	0	0	0	0	0	0	0	0	3	3	1	3	10
ZACAPALA	0	0	0	0	0	0	0	0	0	0	0	0	0	0	5	0	0	3	8
XOCHITLAN	0	0	0	0	0	0	0	0	0	0	0	0	0	1	0	3	0	0	4
GRACIAS	0	0	0	0	0	0	0	0	0	0	0	0	0	0	0	1	1	4	6
EL ZAPOTE	0	0	0	0	0	0	0	3	0	0	0	0	0	0	8	2	2	5	20
TEPEACA	0	0	0	0	0	2	0	0	0	0	0	5	5	5	0	0	0	23	40
OCOTLAN	0	0	0	0	0	1	0	0	1	0	0	2	1	0	0	0	0	0	5
CUAUTEMPAM	0	0	1	1	0	4	3	7	0	0	0	0	1	3	3	3	1	3	30
CALCO	3	2	4	0	7	1	14	42	0	3	2	3	2	12	100	73	25	117	410
HONDO	0	1	0	0	7	7	5	12	6	8	8	9	3	19	35	69	2	4	195
CANAL	0	4	1	1	2	1	2	23	5	5	2	0	22	57	23	0	2	30	180
COMULCO	0	7	5	2	0	1	3	16	4	5	2	1	2	0	21	26	5	1	101
MIMIAPAN	0	0	0	0	6	4	5	9	3	4	1	4	20	22	41	20	10	1	150
AYUTLA	0	0	0	0	0	0	5	0	0	0	0	0	0	0	0	0	0	0	5
COIXTLAHUACA	0	0	0	0	0	0	4	0	0	0	0	0	0	0	0	0	0	6	10
XAMILPAN	0	0	0	0	0	0	2	1	0	0	0	0	0	0	0	0	0	7	10
BALSAS	1	0	0	0	0	0	0	0	0	0	0	0	0	0	0	0	0	10	11
ROSARIO	0	2	1	0	0	0	0	0	0	0	0	0	0	0	0	0	0	1	4
XOLOCHTA	4	11	3	1	0	0	0	0	0	0	0	0	0	0	0	0	0	15	34
COATEPETL	33	111	35	9	8	11	19	43	24	15	13	10	42	73	83	31	76	28	664
IXCAQUISTLA	44	42	20	4	0	0	0	0	0	0	0	0	0	0	0	0	0	28	138
PLUMBATE	0	0	0	0	0	1	0	0	0	0	0	0	0	0	0	4	0	0	5
HUAJUAPAN DOMESTIC THIN ORANGE	0	0	0	0	0	0	0	0	0	0	0	0	3	0	5	2	2	1	13
MIXTEC POLYCHROME	0	0	0	0	0	0	0	0	0	0	0	0	0	0	6	0	0	0	6
ACATLAN POLYCHROME	0	0	0	0	1	1	1	1	0	0	0	1	2	3	0	0	0	23	33
CHOLULA POLYCHROME	9	36	6	3	2	0	1	6	6	2	2	0	2	13	41	26	3	120	278
TEXCOCO MOULDED	0	0	0	0	0	0	0	0	0	0	0	0	5	0	0	0	0	0	5
CULHUACAN BLACK/ORANGE	0	0	0	0	0	0	0	3	0	0	0	1	2	1	2	12	5	15	41
TENOCHTITLAN BLACK/ORANGE	0	0	0	0	0	0	0	0	0	0	0	0	2	5	3	0	0	3	13
TLATELOLCO BLACK/ORANGE	0	7	1	0	0	0	0	0	0	0	0	0	0	0	0	0	0	3	11
TEXCOCO BLACK AND WHITE/RED	1	0	0	0	0	0	0	1	0	0	0	0	0	2	1	0	0	9	14
TEXCOCO BLACK/RED	0	4	0	1	1	0	3	2	1	0	1	1	2	5	6	2	0	50	79
TEXCOCO BLACK/RED INCISED	1	1	0	0	0	0	0	1	0	0	1	0	0	2	2	1	0	19	28
TOTAL	131	276	121	51	64	41	98	250	88	81	59	55	187	431	787	609	519	1413	5261

Brown Painted:Tepexi, Tepeaca Red Painted: Tepeaca, Acatlan Polychrome.

Comparative material: Itzocan, Tehuacan, and Molcaxac collections in the IPAH; Tehuacan-Teotitlan Incised and Coxcatlan Red on Cream (Chadwick and MacNeish, 1967: figs. 72–76).

Incised line or lines parallel to rim: Molcaxac Incised: Molcaxac, Mila Incised:Mila, Tlaltempan Reddish Brown Painted:Tlaltempan.

Comparative material: Itzocan, Tehuacan and Molcaxac collections in the IPAH.

Strap handle: Almolongo Red:Almolongo, Huajoyuca Reddish Yellow:Huajoyuca, Calco Light Red:Calco, Coatepetl Reddish Brown:Coatepetl.

Comparative material: Valley of Mexico (Tolstoy, 1958), Monte Albán V (Caso and Acosta, 1967: figs. 387–388).

Conical support: Almolongo Red:Almolongo, El Zapote Molded:El Zapote, Cholula Polychrome.

Comparative material: Cholula (Noguera, 1954: p. 134); Yagul, Mitla, Monte Albán, Zaachila (Bernal, 1966: p. 355); Acatlan (Seler-Sachs, 1949: p. 109); Valley of Mexico (Tolstoy, 1958: pp. 39, 42, 66, 67), Zautla in the FMNA; Monte Albán V (Caso and Acosta, 1967: fig. 377, pl. XV, no. 9).

Vessel floor deeply incised with parallel lines and parallel crescents: Almolongo Red:Almolongo.

Finger impressions in clay: Almolongo Red:Almolongo.

Comparative material: Monte Albán V (Caso and Acosta, 1967: fig. 383a).

Griddle with ridged rim: Almolongo Red:Almolongo, Huajoyuca Reddish Yellow:Huajoyuca, Ixcaquistla Speckled:Ixcaquistla, Comulco Gray:Comulco.

Comparative material: Ixcaquistla (Landa Abrego, 1966: personal communication); Itzocan, Huehuetlan collections in the IPAH.

Nubbin appendage: Huajoyuca Reddish Yellow:Huajoyuca, Tepexi Brown Painted:Tepexi.

Comparative material: Huehuetlan, Molcaxac, Chiquihuite, San Francisco de Asis Tetla (Totimehuacan) collections in the IPAH.

Base with rounded obtuse angle: Tepexi Brown Painted:Tepexi, Tepeaca Red Painted:Tepeaca.

Comparative material: Huehuetlan, Molcaxac, Chiquihuite, San Francisco de Asis Tetla (Totimehuacan) collections in the IPAH; Yanhuitlan and Nochistlan collections in the AMNH; Valley of Mexico (Tolstoy, 1958).

Painted undulating lines paralleling rim: Tepexi Brown Painted:Tepexi, Zacapala Dark Brown Painted: Zacapala, Tepeaca Red Painted:Tepeaca, Tlaltempan Reddish Brown Painted:Tlaltempan, Cholula Polychrome.

Comparative material: Tepeaca, Huehuetlan, Tepozuchil, Molcaxac, Chiquihuite, San Francisco de Asis Tetla (Totimehuacan) collections in the IPAH;

Yanhuitlan and Nochistlan collections in the AMNH; Cholula (Noguera, 1954).

Painted straight lines paralleling rim: Tepexi Brown Painted:Tepexi, Zacapala Dark Brown Painted: Zacapala, Tlaltempan Reddish Brown Painted: Tlaltempan, Balsas Red Painted:Balsas.

Comparative material: Tepeaca, Huehuetlan, Molcaxac, Chiquihuite, Tepozuchil, San Francisco de Asis Tetla (Totimehuacan) collections in the IPAH; Yanhuitlan and Nochistlan collections in the AMNH; Zautla in the FMNH; Tehuacan-Coxcatlan Red on Cream (Chadwick and MacNeish, 1967: fig. 76).

Painted rim band: Tepexi Brown Painted:Tepexi, Zacapala Dark Brown Painted:Zacapala, Tepeaca Red Painted.Tepeaca, Tlaltempan Reddish Brown Painted:Tlaltempan, Balsas Red Painted:Balsas, Acatlan Polychrome.

Comparative material: Tepeaca, Huehuetlan, Molcaxac, Chiquihuite, San Francisco de Asis Tetla (Totimehuacan), Tepozuchil, Yanhuitlan, Nochistlan collections in the AMNH; Cuicatlan, Jayacatlan, Coixtlahuaca, Santa Maria Ixcatlan, Acatlan, Calipan,

TABLE 2

CHI SQUARE VALUES

	CCHSQ
TLALTEMPAN	8.24
MOLCAXAC	5.59
ALMOLONGO	36.91
CHOCHOS	52.29
HUAJOYUCA	47.04
TEPEXI	16.46
YAGUL	9.34
MILA	3.63
ZACAPALA	2.60
XOCHITLAN	2.08
GRACIAS	1.04
EL ZAPOTE	4.68
TEPEACA	13.93
OCOTLAN	21.48
CUAUTEMPAM	42.46
CALCO	63.58
HONDO	50.50
CANAL	18.59
COMULCO	10.88
MIMIAPAN	27.17
AYUTLA	37.47
COIXTLAHUACA	29.98
XAMILPAN	22.48
BALSAS	5.65
ROSARIO	16.94
XOLOCHTA	107.27
COATEPETL	125.34
IXCAQUISTLA	621.05
PLUMBATE	1.56
HUAJUAPAN DOMESTIC THIN ORANGE	6.23
MIXTEC POLYCHROME	3.11
ACATLAN POLYCHROME	8.75
CHOLULA POLYCHROME	47.08
TEXCOCO MOULDED	2.60
CULHUACAN BLACK/ORANGE	5.74
TENOCHTITLAN BLACK/ORANGE	5.19
TLATELOLCO BLACK/ORANGE	45.17
TEXCOCO BLACK AND WHITE/RED	0.76
TEXCOCO BLACK/RED	3.28
TEXCOCO BLACK/RED INCISED	0.63

Cholula, Culhuacan (Seler-Sachs, 1949; Espejo, 1949).

Painted spiral motif: Tepexi Brown Painted:Tepexi, Zacapala Dark Brown Painted:Zacapala, Balsas Red Painted:Balsas, Cholula Polychrome.

Comparative material: Tepeaca, Molcaxac, Chiquihuite, Huehuetlan, Tepozuchil, San Francisco de Asis Tetla (Totimehuacan) collections in the IPAH; Yanhuitlan, Nochistlan collections in the AMNH, Zaachila (Paddock, 1966), Cholula (Noguera, 1954).

Mica temper: Ixcaquistla Speckled:Ixcaquistla, Cuautempan Silvery:Cuautempan, Xochitlan Chalky Slip: Xochitlan, Mimiapan Black:Mimiapan.

Comparative material: Ixcaquistla (Landa Abrego, 1966: personal communication), Valley of Mexico (Tolstoy, 1958).

Heavily tempered with coarse to granular particles: Chochos Red:Chochos, Xochitlan Chalky Slip:Xochitlan, Ayutla Red/Gray:Ayutla.

Bifurcate nubbin support: Coatepetl Reddish Brown: Coatepetl.

Comparative material: Calipan (Noguera, 1940: pl. 22).

Lustrous black or dark gray slip: Canal Black:Canal, Mila Incised:Mila, Coixtlahuaca Black, Xolochta Finely Incised:Xolochta.

Comparative material: Tehuacan collection in the IPAH, Coixtlahuaca (Bernal, 1948–1949: pp. 42,

TABLE 3

PROPORTION OF CERAMIC GROUPS, WARES, AND TYPES IN EACH PHASE

	TOYNA	XAOUA UNMIXED	XAOUA MIXED PCTOFPH	HUICHI	TOTAL
TLALTEMPAN	0.0052	0.0066	0.021	0.0063	0.0073
MOLCAXAC	0.0017	0.0044	0.0071	0.0012	0.0021
ALMOLONGO	0.11	0.17	0.18	0.23	0.2
CHOCHOS	0.11	0.031	0.046	0.14	0.12
HUAJOYUCA	0.04	0.088	0.17	0.14	0.12
TEPEXI	0.0017	0.029	0.014	0.029	0.024
YAGUL	0	0	0	0.0071	0.0047
MILA	0	0	0	0.0028	0.0018
ZACAPALA	0	0	0	0.002	0.0013
XOCHITLAN	0	0	0	0.0016	0.001
GRACIAS	0	0	0	0.00079	0.00052
EL ZAPOTE	0	0.0066	0	0.0047	0.0039
TEPEACA	0	0.0044	0.018	0.0039	0.0044
OCOTLAN	0	0.0022	0.011	0.00039	0.0013
CUAUTEMPAM	0.0035	0.031	0	0.0043	0.007
CALCO	0.016	0.14	0.028	0.084	0.076
HONDO	0.0017	0.068	0.11	0.051	0.05
CANAL	0.01	0.062	0.042	0.041	0.039
COMULCO	0.024	0.044	0.042	0.021	0.026
MIMIAPAN	0	0.053	0.042	0.045	0.039
AYUTLA	0	0.011	0	0	0.0013
COIXTLAHUACA	0	0.0088	0	0	0.001
XAMILPAN	0	0.0066	0	0	0.00078
BALSAS	0.0017	0	0	0	0.00026
ROSARIO	0.0052	0	0	0	0.00078
XOLOCHTA	0.033	0	0	0	0.0049
COATEPETL	0.32	0.18	0.22	0.12	0.17
IXCAQUISTLA	0.19	0	0	0	0.029
PLUMBATE	0	0.0022	0	0.0016	0.0013
HUAJUAPAN DOMESTIC THIN ORANGE	0	0	0	0.0047	0.0031
MIXTEC POLYCHROME	0	0	0	0.0024	0.0016
ACATLAN POLYCHROME	0	0.0088	0.0035	0.002	0.0026
CHOLULA POLYCHROME	0.093	0.02	0.035	0.034	0.041
TEXCOCO MOULDED	0	0	0	0.002	0.0013
CULHUACAN BLACK/ORANGE	0	0.0066	0.0035	0.0087	0.0068
TENOCHTITLAN BLACK/ORANGE	0	0	0	0.0039	0.0026
TLATELOLCO BLACK/ORANGE	0.014	0	0	0	0.0021
TEXCOCO BLACK AND WHITE/RED	0.0017	0.0022	0	0.0012	0.0013
TEXCOCO BLACK/RED	0.0086	0.013	0.011	0.0059	0.0075
TEXCOCO BLACK/RED INCISED	0.0035	0.0022	0.0035	0.002	0.0023
TOTAL	1	1	1	1	1

44), Tehuacan-Teotitlan Incised (Chadwick and MacNeish, 1967: figs. 70, 72).

Silty texture: Tepeaca Red Painted:Tepeaca, Balsas Red Painted:Balsas, Hondo Grayish Brown:Hondo, Coixtlahuaca Black:Coixtlahuaca, Zacapala Dark Brown Painted:Zacapala.

Comparative material: Coixtlahuaca (Bernal, 1948–1949: pp. 42, 44); Tepeaca, Huehuetlan collections in the IPAH; Yanhuitlan, Nochistlan collections in the AMNH.

Present in Huichi Phase Only

Light gray slip on compact surface: Yagul Gray:Yagul.

Comparative material: Coixtlahuaca (Bernal, 1948–1949: pp. 41–42), Yagul (*Mesoamerican Notes,* 1955: p. 74).

Lateral perforations in support forming triangle: El Zapote Molded:El Zapote.

Comparative material: Tepozuchil collection in the IPAH.

Triangular support: Zacapala Dark Brown Painted: Zacapala.

Comparative material: Tepozuchil collection in the IPAH, Zautla in the FMNH.

Lustrous white surface: Various unidentified polychromes.

Comparative material: Tlanhualpa-Tajin Polished White, Tuxpilla (Ekholm, 1953), Tihuatlan, Tabuco collections in the AMNH, Totonacapan (Medellin, 1960: pp. 149–158).

Painted long parallel vertical lines: Zacapala Dark Brown Painted: Zacapala.

TABLE 4

RANK OF CERAMIC GROUPS, WARES, AND TYPES IN EACH PHASE

	TOYNA	XAQUA		HUICHI	TOTAL
		UNMIXED	MIXED		
TLALTEMPAN	13	17	11	14	14
MOLCAXAC	17	21	16	29	25
ALMOLONGO	3	2	2	1	1
CHOCHOS	4	9	5	2	4
HUAJOYUCA	6	4	3	3	3
TEPEXI	18	11	13	10	12
YAGUL	22	27	20	13	18
MILA	23	28	21	21	27
ZACAPALA	24	29	22	23	29
XOCHITLAN	25	30	23	27	35
GRACIAS	26	31	24	31	39
EL ZAPOTE	27	18	25	16	20
TEPEACA	28	22	12	19	19
OCOTLAN	29	23	14	32	30
CUAUTEMPAM	15	10	26	18	15
CALCO	9	3	10	5	5
HONDO	19	5	4	6	6
CANAL	11	6	6	8	8
COMULCO	8	8	7	11	11
MIMIAPAN	30	7	8	7	9
AYUTLA	31	14	27	33	31
COIXTLAHUACA	32	15	28	34	36
XAMILPAN	33	19	29	35	37
BALSAS	20	32	30	36	40
ROSARIO	14	33	31	37	38
XOLOCHTA	7	34	32	38	17
COATEPETL	1	1	1	4	2
IXCAQUISTLA	2	35	33	39	10
PLUMBATE	34	24	34	28	32
HUAJUAPAN DOMESTIC THIN ORANGE	35	36	35	17	21
MIXTEC POLYCHROME	36	37	36	22	28
ACATLAN POLYCHROME	37	16	17	24	22
CHOLULA POLYCHROME	5	12	9	9	7
TEXCOCO MOULDED	38	38	37	25	33
CULHUACAN BLACK/ORANGE	39	20	18	12	16
TENOCHTITLAN BLACK/ORANGE	40	39	38	20	23
TLATELOLCO BLACK/ORANGE	10	40	39	40	26
TEXCOCO BLACK AND WHITE/RED	21	25	40	30	34
TEXCOCO BLACK/RED	12	13	15	15	13
TEXCOCO BLACK/RED INCISED	16	26	19	26	24

Comparative material: Tepozuchil collection in the
IPAH.
Incised short parallel vertical lines: Mila Incised:Mila.
Chalky white slip: Xochitlan Chalky Slip:Xochitlan.
Comparative material: Mixtec collection (sites uni-
identified) in the MNA.
Painted short parallel vertical lines: Zacapala Dark
Brown Painted:Zacapala.
Comparative material: Tepozuchil collection in the
IPAH; Mixtec collection (sites unidentified) in the
MNA; Yanhuitlan, Nochistlan collections in the
AMNH.

Present in the Huichi and Xaqua Phases

*Molded geometric motifs on vessel floor and lower
inner walls:* El Zapote Molded:El Zapote, Acatlan
Polychrome.
Comparative material: Chiquihuite, Tepozuchil, Mol-
caxac collections in the IPAH, Cuicatlan, Jayacatlan,
Coixtlahuaca, Santa Maria Ixcatlan, Culhuacan,
Acatlan (Espejo, 1949; Seler-Sachs, 1949); Acatlan
(Franco, 1955; Moser, 1969); Calipan (Noguera,
1940); Cholula (Noguera, 1954).
Incised horizontal lines on neck interior: Tlaltempan
Reddish Brown Painted:Tlaltempan.
*Cross-cutting horizontal and vertical parallel lines with
circles:* Acatlan Polychrome, Canal Black:Canal.
Comparative material: Cuicatlan, Jayacatlan, Coixtla-
. huaca, Santa Maria Ixcatlan, Acatlan, Calipan,
Cholula, Culhuacan (Espejo, 1949; Seler-Sachs,
1949); Acatlan (Franco, 1955, Moser, 1969);
Tehuacan-Teotitlan Incised (Chadwick and Mac-
Neish, 1967: fig. 72).
Crenelated slab support: Acatlan Polychrome, Xamil-
pan Pink/Brown:Xamilpan.
Comparative material: Cuicatlan, Jayacatlan, Coixtlahuaca, Santa Maria Ixcatlan, Acatlan, Culhuacan
(Seler-Sachs, 1949; Espejo, 1949); Calipan (No-
guera, 1940); Cholula (Noguera, 1954); Monte
Albán V (Caso and Acosta, 1967: pl. XVI); Valley
of Mexico (Tolstoy, 1958); Tehuacan-Teotitlan In-
cised and Coxcatlan Gray (Chadwick and MacNeish,
1967: figs. 73, 75).
Use of graphite for decoration: Ocotlan Graphite:Ocot-
lan.
Comparative material: Yagul (*Mesoamerican Notes,*
1955: fig. 21); Coixtlahuaca, Zaachila (Bernal
1966a: p. 355); Chalco (O'Neill, 1962).
Painted undulating lines diagonal to rim: Tepeaca Red
Painted:Tepeaca.
Comparative material: Tehuacan-Coxcatlan Red on
Cream (Chadwick and MacNeish, 1967: fig. 76).
Painted fret: Tepeaca Red Painted:Tepeaca, Tepexi
Brown Painted:Tepexi.
Comparative material:Mixtec collection (sites unidenti-
fied) in the MNA; Zaachila, Yagul (Paddock, 1966:
pls. 18–21, 32, 34, 36, 38). Tehuacan-Coxcatlan

Red on Cream (Chadwick and MacNeish, 1967: fig.
70).
Wide band parallel to neck with motifs therein: Canal
Black:Canal.
Comparative material: Tehuacan-Teotitlan Incised
(Chadwick and MacNeish, 1967: fig. 72).

Present in the Xaqua phase only

Painted lip band: Xamilpan Pink/Brown Xamilpan,
Ayutla Red/Gray:Ayutla.
Painted bottom of support: Xamilpan Pink/Brown:
Xamilpan.

Present in Huichi and Toyna Phases

Incised undulating line motif: Mila Incised:Mila
Xolochta Finely Incised:Xolochta.
Painted paired short vertical lines: Mixtec Polychrome,
Balsas Red Painted:Balsas.
Comparative material: Mixtec collection (sites uni-
dentified) in the MNA.

Present in the Toyna Phase Only

Flattened cylindrical handle: Ixcaquistla Speckled:
Ixcaquistla.
Painted step-fret: Balsas Red Painted:Balsas, Cholula
Polychrome.
Comparative material: Mixtec collections (sites uni-
dentified) in the MNA, Cholula (Noguera, 1954).
Incised spiral: Xolochta Finely Incised:Xolochta.
Painted neck band: Rosario Black/Red.

FIG. 23. Three spindle whorls and a bead. Scale 1:1.

FIG. 24. Head with zoomorphic and anthropomorphic features full view, profile view, head of man. Scale 1:1

Hollowed cylindrical handle: Xolochta Finely Incised: Xolochta.

Comparative material: Calipan (Noguera, 1940: pl. 29, fig. 1).

Zoomorphic support: Cholula Polychrome.

Comparative material: Cholula (Noguera, 1954), Monte Albán V (Caso and Acosta, 1967: fig. 376, plates XIV, XIX), Tehuacan-Teotitlan Incised (Chadwick and MacNeish, 1967: fig. 73), Mixteca Alta (Caso and Bernal, 1965: pp. 862–863).

Other ceramic artifacts (none found in stratified deposits except the last two):

Perforated clay disk: Comparative material: La Ladrillera, Early Classic (Delgado, 1961: p. 97), Tehuantepec-Early Classic (Wallrath, 1967: fig. 78g).

Adornment representing a flower: Comparative material: Monte Albán-Classic (Caso and Bernal, 1952: fig. 28a) Teotihuacan-Classic (Gamio, 1922: pl. 110b), Tehuantepec-late Late Classic (Wallrath, 1967: fig. 77u).

Perforated beads, cylindrical, with and without painted decoration.

Female figure: (fragment). Comparative material: Possibly Tula (Franco, 1965: personal communication), (Noguera, 1965: fig. 33a, no. 17).

Small balls, diameter, 15–17 mm.

Spindle whorls (fig. 23): One mold made, all undecorated and made of paste with silty texture. Comparative material: Spindle whorls are extremely rare in the Valley of Oaxaca and common in the Mixteca Alta (Bernal, 1965: p. 807), Caso and Bernal, 1965: pp. 894–895). Also common at Cholula (Noguera, 1954).

Figure of seated drummer: (fragment). Comparative material: Aztec IV (Franco, 1965: personal communication).

Head with zoomorphic and anthropomorphic features (fig. 24): (fragment).

Stamped clay fragment with some incising: Found in Xaqua stratum.

Head of man (fig. 24): (fragment) with white undercoat and fugitive polychrome paint. Found in Huichi phase stratum. Comparative material: Oaxaca, Central Mexico (Paddock: personal communication).

STONE

The vast majority of stone artifacts are chipped. Most were not found in stratified deposits and so do not contribute information on chronological periods during the occupation of Tepexi. The number found in stratified deposits is too small for any valid statistical analyses. The chart of the stone artifacts simply lists type and quantity.

In the following discussion the terminology is based on the work of Epstein (1964), Tolstoy (n.d.), and MacNeish and others (1967).

FLAKES
Trimming Flakes
(fig. 25)

Total number of specimens: 913.

Material: 789 chert, 88 obsidian, 34 quartzite, 2 basalt.

Dimensions: length: 1.5 cm.–5.9 cm., width: 1.1 cm.–4.1 cm., thickness: 0.2 cm.–1.6 cm.

They are generally polyhedral, roughly rectangular or fan-shaped. There is no indication of retouch on these flakes. However, 299 chert, 38 obsidian, 17 quartzite, and 2 basalt flakes have nicks and striations which suggest casual use, but these may be due to other causes. These flakes are the by-products of tool

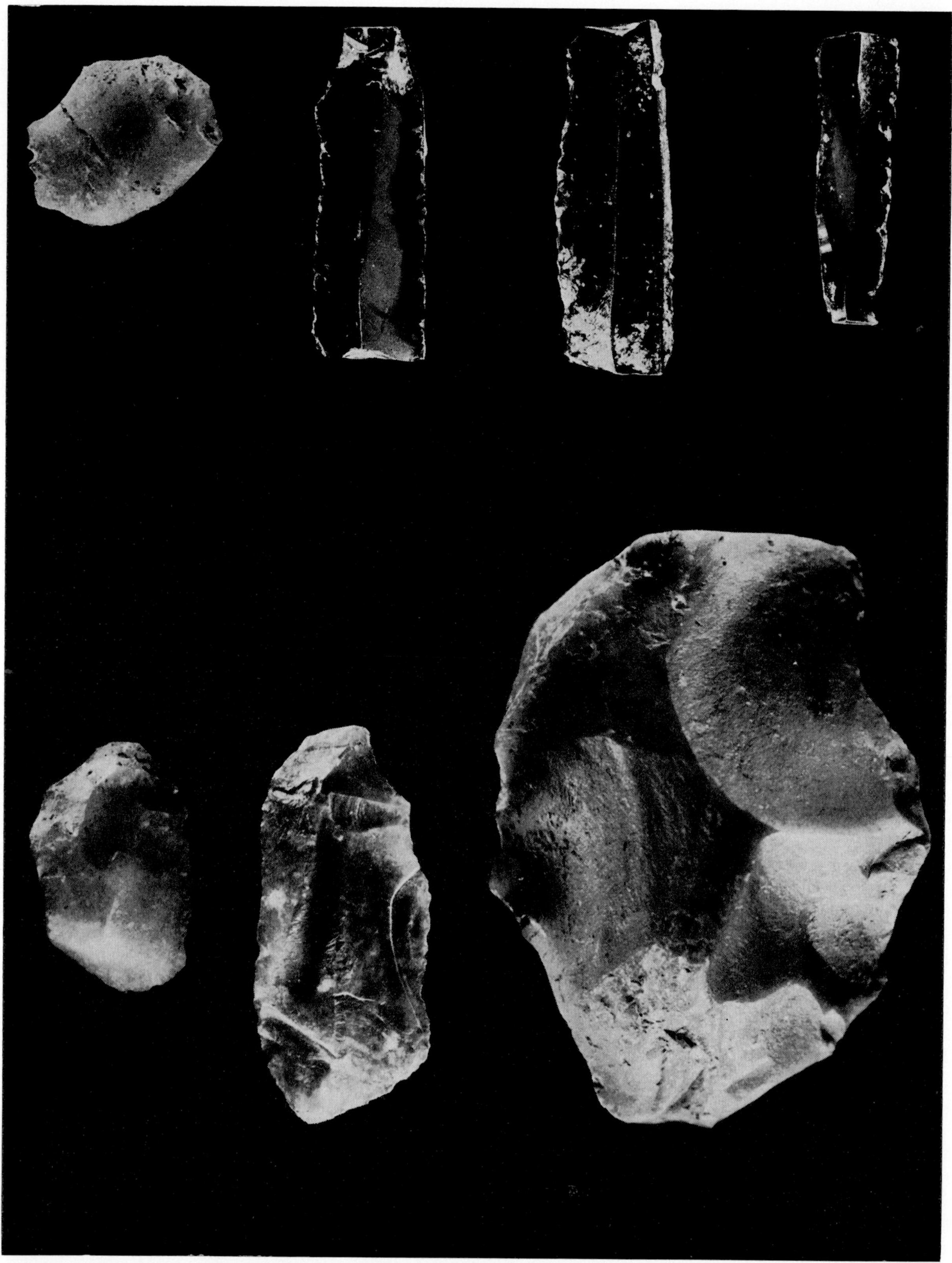

FIG. 25. Top row: Trimming flake, Fine blade, terminal end snapped, Fine blade, both ends snapped, Fine blade, bulbar end snapped. Bottom row: Crude blade, prepared striking platform, Crude blade, pointed striking platform, Crude cylindrical nucleus. Scale 1.25 : 1

manufacture, and may themselves have been used as tools.

BLADES

Blades are defined, following MacNeish and others (1967: p. 17) as "... chipped stone tools with roughly parallel lateral edges, a dorsal surface divided by one or more lengthwise ridges, and an unworked ventral surface, usually with a bulb of percussion near the end adjacent to the remains of the striking platform." In this collection there are fine blades and crude blades.

Fine Blades
(fig. 25)

Total number of specimens: 218.
Material: 218 obsidian.
Dimensions: length: 1.0 cm.–4.5 cm., width: 0.8 cm.–2.0 cm., thickness: 0.2 cm.–0.7 cm.

Fine blades have single or double parallel dorsal medial ridges, a slightly concave ventral surface, a slight bulb of percussion, and are prismatic in cross section. They all appear to have been struck from fluted or bullet-shaped cores, and have ground striking platforms. There is not a single whole fine blade in the collection. All have been snapped, that is, either one or both ends of the blade appear to have been deliberately snapped off.

Seventy-six of the blades have the terminal end snapped off. The dimensions of these blades are: length: 1.2 cm.–4.5 cm., width: 0.8 cm.–2.0 cm., thickness: 0.2 cm.–0.7 cm.

One hundred and twenty-seven blades have both ends snapped off. The dimensions of these blades are: length: 1.0 cm.–4.0 cm., width: 0.8 cm.–1.8 cm., thickness: 0.2 cm.–0.5 cm.

Fifteen blades have the bulbar end snapped off, and the terminal end remains. The dimensions of these blades are: length: 1.6 cm.–3.7 cm., width: 0.8 cm.–1.3 cm., thickness: 0.2 cm.–0.3 cm.

MacNeish and others (1967: pp. 24–25) have suggested that the snapped blades, that is, according to his usage, blades with *both* ends broken off, were inserted into handles. In order for a blade to fit firmly into a slotted holder, it must have a straight profile. The terminal end, which curves to form a concave ventral surface, must be broken off. The bulb of percussion of fine blades with ground striking platforms is not well-defined and offers no hindrance in setting the blade into the handle. I would suggest, therefore, that both the fine blades with bulbar end remaining and terminal end snapped, and the fine blades with two snapped ends were able to be set in handles. The 15 fine blades with only the terminal end remaining are probably the by-products of the production of snapped blades.

Neither the edges nor ends of these fine blades are retouched. The sharpness of obsidian is dulled by re-touch and the sharpest edge for cutting is unretouched. Nicks and striations on the blades appear to be equal on both lateral edges. This may be a result of changing blades from one side of the handle to the other, a practice which would ensure that both edges were used.

Fine blades have a wide temporal and spatial distribution in Mesoamerica.

Crude Blades
(fig. 25)

Total number of specimens: 69.
Material: 63 chert, 6 obsidian.
Dimensions: length: 1.7 cm.–6.6 cm., width: 1.0 cm.–3.3 cm., thickness: 0.2 cm.–1.4 cm.

There are two kinds of crude blades in this collection: those with prepared striking platforms and those with pointed striking platforms. MacNeish and others (1967: p. 20) have described crude blades with prepared striking platforms as ranging "... in outline from rectangles to long narrow triangles, with a long oblong form the most prevalent. Lateral edges vary from slightly convex and the opposite end varies from straight to almost pointed and is most often convex. Ventral surfaces are generally concave, with a well-marked bulb of percussion near the striking platform."

There are 18 crude blades with prepared striking platforms in the Tepexi collection. Their dimensions are: length: 1.9 cm.–6.6 cm.; width: 2.2 cm.–3.3 cm.; thickness: 0.3 cm.–1.4 cm.

Crude blades with pointed striking platforms are described by MacNeish and others (1967: p. 21) as "... predominately long and leaf or lance shaped.... Ventral surfaces vary from slightly convex to definitely concave, with the majority being slightly concave. [There is no] ... well-marked bulb of percussion. Striking platforms are difficult to discern and very small, but they show evidence of working and are roughly oval to pointed in shape. They seem to be at right angles to the dorsal surface. Dorsal surfaces usually have a single medial ridge roughly parallel to the lateral edges; many of these ridges are rather wavy."

There are 27 crude blades with pointed striking platforms. Their dimensions are: length: 2.3 cm.–6.4 cm.; width: 1.0 cm.–2.9 cm.; thickness: 0.3 cm.–0.9 cm.

There are also 24 snapped blades. All these blades are snapped at both ends. The dimensions are: length: 1.7 cm.–3.3 cm.; width: 1.1 cm.–1.7 cm.; thickness: 0.2 cm.–0.7 cm.

Crude blades appear in greater number in Tepexi than in the Venta Salada phase (which is contemporary with the Tepexi phases) at Tehuacan, and in far greater proportion. At Tehuacan crude blades were more numerous in the earlier El Riego, the Coxcatlan, and the Abejas phases than in the Venta Salada phase (MacNeish and others, 1967: pp. 20–21).

CORES

Crude Cylindrical Nuclei
(fig. 25)

Total number of specimens: 3.
Material: 3 chert.

Dimensions: length: 4.0 cm.–7.2 cm., diameter: 2.7 cm.–4.6 cm.

The type has been described by MacNeish and others (1967: p. 27). (It is) ". . . made from a roughly cylindrical nodule. . . . Indirect percussion applied to the striking platforms at the end or ends of the

Fig. 26. Top row: Graver on a point, Fine bullet shaped nucleus.   Blade spokeshave.
Bottom row: Quartzite side scraper.   Scale 1 : 1/2.

cylinders produces two to four flutes along the sides. The spalls scaled off the sides probably were of the type crude blades with pointed striking platforms."

The specimens from Tepexi have one striking platform. MacNeish and others comment that the two specimens of this type which he found in excavation belong to the Coxcatlan and Abejas phases. As with crude blades, crude cylindrical nuclei are in far greater proportion at Tepexi than in the Venta Salada phase which is contemporary with the Tepexi phases.

Fine Bullet-Shaped Nuclei
(fig. 26)

Total number of specimens: 2.
Material: 2 obsidian.
Dimensions: length: 3.0 cm.–6.3 cm., diameter: 1.3 cm.–2.3 cm.

These are cylindrical cores from whose sides long, parallel flakes were removed producing a fluted surface. One specimen is a fragment with the striking platform missing: the other has an unprepared striking platform. These fine bullet-shaped nuclei are widely distributed in Mesoamerica in time and space.

FACIALLY TRIMMED ARTIFACTS

Blade Spokeshaves
(fig. 26)

Total number of specimens: 7.
Material: 7 obsidian.
Dimensions: length: 1.8 cm.–3.2 cm.; width: 1.0 cm.–1.5 cm.; thickness: 0.3 cm.–0.5 cm.; notch length: 0.5 cm.–0.9 cm.; notch width: 0.2 cm.–0.3 cm.
Indicated use: spokeshave.

These are snapped fine blades with retouched notches on one edge.

Blade Side Scrapers
(fig. 27)

Total number of specimens: 3.
Material: 3 obsidian.
Dimensions: length: 2.3 cm.–4.0 cm.; width: 0.9 cm.–1.6 cm.; thickness: 0.2 cm.–0.4 cm.
Indicated use: scrapers.

These are fine blades with unifacially retouched lateral edges.

Blade End Scrapers
(fig. 27)

Total number of specimens: 8.
Material: 8 obsidian.
Dimensions: length: 2.4 cm.–6.6 cm.; width: 1.1 cm.–1.9 cm.; thickness: 0.2 cm.–0.9 cm.
Indicated use: scrapers.

These are fine blades with unifacially retouched ends. They appear throughout the Tehuacan sequence, in the ceramic phases of the Valley of Mexico, in the

Santa Marta Complex in Chiapas, and in the Eslabones and Los Angeles phases at Tamaulipas (MacNeish and others, 1967: pp. 41–42, Tolstoy n.d., MacNeish, 1958: p. 81, table 4).

Flake Side Scrapers
(figs. 26, 27)

Total number of specimens: 2.
Material: 1 obsidian, 1 quartzite.
Dimensions of obsidian flake: length: 4.3 cm.; width: 2.5 cm.; thickness: 0.3 cm.
Dimensions of quartzite flake: diameter: 4.2 cm.; thickness: 1.5 cm.
Indicated use: scrapers.

The obsidian flake is thin and trapezoidal with the ventral surface flat and unworked. The dorsal surface is pressure-retouched along one lateral edge. This type of artifact is found in all phases at Tamaulipas (MacNeish, 1958: p. 78, fig. 26–3), and Tehuacan (MacNeish and others, 1967: pp. 50–51).

The quartzite flake is discoidal in shape and has flake scars on both the ventral and dorsal surfaces. One dorsal edge is retouched. They are dated from Tlatilco time onward in the Valley of Mexico (Tolstoy, n.d.: pp. 22, 23), and resemble the thick flake—one edge retouched type in all phases at Tehuacan (MacNeish and others, 1967: p. 50).

Flake Spokeshaves
(fig. 27)

Total number of specimens: 5.
Material: 3 obsidian, 2 chert.
Dimensions: length: 2.4 cm.–5.2 cm.; width: 1.8 cm.–3.9 cm.; thickness: 0.6 cm.–2.4 cm.; notch length: 0.4 cm.–1.3 cm.; notch width: 0.4 cm.–0.9 cm.
Indicated use: spokeshaves.

Similar tools have been found throughout the Tamaulipas (MacNeish, 1958: p. 79) and Tehuacan sequences although, apparently, they have not been noted for the rest of Mexico (MacNeish and others, 1967: p. 47).

Flake Gravers
(fig. 27)

Total number of specimens: 13.
Material: 3 obsidian, 10 chert.
Dimensions of 12 specimens: length: 1.6 cm.–3.7 cm.; width: 0.7 cm.– 2.3 cm.; thickness: 0.3 cm.–0.9 cm.
Dimensions of 1 specimen (considerably larger than the rest): length: 5.6 cm.; width: 4.1 cm.
Indicated use: gravers.

These flakes are of varying shapes although a general rectangular shape is most common. They are characterized by a small sharp point formed by pressure retouch usually at the junction of an edge and an end. Except for the largest, all specimens show flake scars on the dorsal surface only. Flake gravers resembling these have been found in the Lerma phase at Tamaulipas (MacNeish, 1958: p. 86) and MacNeish has noted that they appear in early horizons in the Great Plains and Southwest of the United States. They do, however, appear throughout the sequence in Tehuacan (MacNeish and others, 1967: p. 47).

Graver on a Point
(fig. 26)

Total number of specimens: 1.
Material: 1 chert.

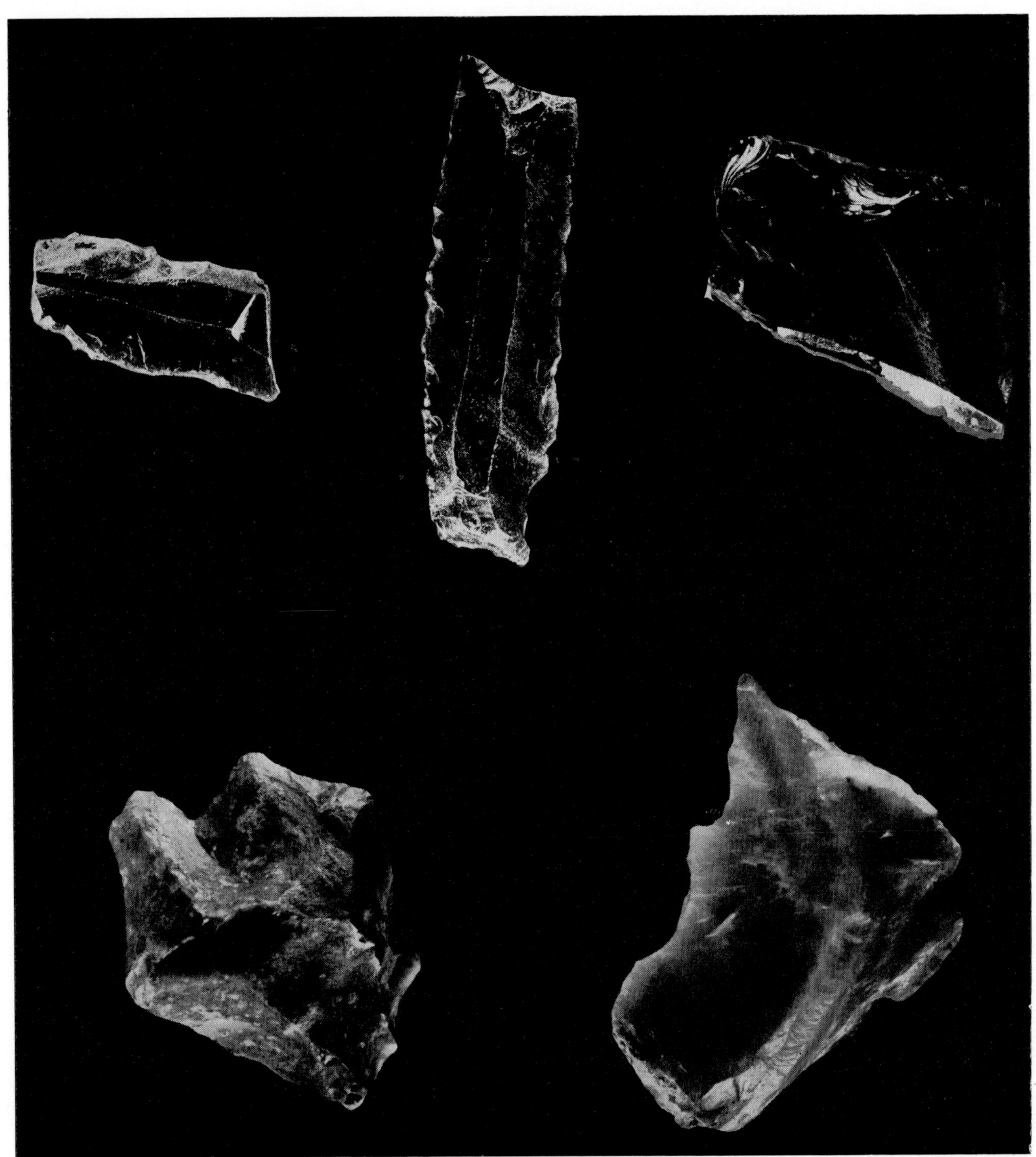

FIG. 27.   Top row: Blade side scraper, Blade end scraper, Obsidian side scraper.
Bottom row: Flake spokeshave, Flake graver.   Scale 1.25 : 1.

Dimensions: length: 5.0 cm., width: 2.1 cm.
Indicated use: graver.

This graver on a point (see below for definition of a point) is a fragment. A completed point (the type is not identifiable) was snapped deliberately, accidentally, or by use, and a sharp nib was formed by pressure retouch at the junction of an edge and an end.

POINTS

Total number of specimens: 33.
Material: 21 chert, 12 obsidian.
Dimensions: length: 1.8 cm.–7.5 cm.; width: 1.0 cm.–3.9 cm.; thickness: 0.15 cm.–0.9 cm.

Points are defined as flat, bifacially trimmed artifacts, generally symmetrical, with a point at one end and with the opposite end trimmed to permit hafting. The large points in this collection (over 4.5 cm. in length) are thicker and heavier and were probably used on darts, spears, and lances. The small points (under 3 cm. in length) are thinner and lighter and were undoubtedly used on arrows as heads. They are unusually small for arrow heads. At Tepexi tiny heads may have been more effective than the usual size arrow heads. Given the same bow, a smaller arrow head will penetrate deeper than a larger. The wound, however, is smaller. But the size of the wound was apparently not critical in killing the victim. Poison seems to have been used in the Mixteca (Dahlgren, 1954: pp. 204–206) and may have been used at Tepexi. The archer, then, was successful in bringing down his victim once the arrow head reached the blood stream. Thus, the tiny arrow heads served to transport the poison to the circulatory system better than the larger (see Pope, 1962: p. 56).

While the bow and arrow are rarely portrayed in the codices (the only exception, apparently, is the Codex Bodley where they are shown frequently) (Dahlgren, 1954: p. 195) they were probably important at Tepexi. The fortifications at Tepexi demanded the use of a long-range weapon such as the bow and arrow. The walls were as many as 15 meters high, and firing probably began when the attackers were on the hillslopes, a distance of 100 meters from the top of the walls.

A drawing from the *Historia Tolteca Chichimeca* (1947: lam.XXIV), illustrating the conquest of Quauhtinchan by the Tlatelolcocas, shows the attacking warriors firing arrows from far below the walls. The great distance is indicated by the position of the arrow perpendicular to the ground, and by the backward thrust of the bowman's head as he aims upward. The defenders respond with the same weapon.

Texcoco
(fig. 28)

Total number of specimens: 7.
Material: 7 chert.
Dimensions: length: 2.8 cm.–7.0 cm.; width: (maximum width is just above the side notches) 2.4 cm.–3.4 cm.; thickness: 0.3 cm.–0.4 cm.; notch length: 0.7 cm.; notch width: 0.5 cm.

Two of the specimens are complete, one was not completed but can be identified as an example of the Texcoco type, and four are fragments. They have tapering, straight or slightly convex edges, a straight or slightly concave base, and notches just above the base. Both surfaces show irregular flaking, and the edges, including the edges of the notches, were pressure retouched. Two of the fragmentary specimens have their pointed ends snapped off. This may have occurred when the weapon was extricated.

Two specimens were found in Huichi phase levels. The Texcoco point has been found in Postclassic horizons in the Valley of Mexico (Tolstoy, n.d.: pp. 18–19) and Tehuacan (MacNeish and others, 1967: pp. 76–77). It resembles the Ensor point found in both Classic and Postclassic horizons at Tamaulipas (MacNeish, 1958: pp. 67–68, fig. 24–17). It is possible that a reevaluation of the Ensor type at Tamaulipas would show it to include both Ensor and Texcoco types with the former appearing in Classic horizons and the latter in Postclassic.

Harrell
(fig. 29)

Total number of specimens: 6.
Material: 3 chert, 3 obsidian.
Dimensions: length: 2.1 cm.–3.0 cm.; width (maximum width is at the base): 1.1 cm.–1.7 cm.; thickness: 0.3 cm.–0.4 cm.; notch length: 0.2 cm.–0.3 cm.; notch width: 0.1 cm.–0.2 cm.
Indicated use: arrow heads.

Both surfaces show irregular delicate flake scars, and the edges show tiny flake scars produced by pressure retouch. They have straight, or in one case, convex tapering edges, a broad stem, notches above the stem, and a straight, concave, or notched base.

According to MacNeish and others (1967: p. 77), Harrell points are widespread in North America in earlier periods than the Mesoamerican Postclassic. They do not appear in the Tehuacan sequence or in the Valley of Mexico (Tolstoy, n.d.: 18–19) until the Postclassic.

Teotihuacan
(fig. 28)

Total number of specimens: 5.
Material: 5 obsidian.
Dimensions: length: 2.1 cm.–2.3 cm.; width (maximum width is at the base): 1.1 cm.–1.4 cm.; thickness: 0.3 cm.–0.4 cm.; notch length: 0.2 cm.; notch width: 0.1 cm.–0.15 cm.
Indicated use: arrow heads.

There are 3 whole and 2 fragmentary specimens.

The specimens in this collection are in the form of an isosceles triangle with notches 2.2 cm. above the straight base. They were made on blades, and where the flaking on the dorsal surface has not been obliterated, the ridge or ridges are visible. Irregular flaking is confined primarily to the dorsal surface, but there

Fig. 28. Top row: Texcoco point, Teotihuacan point, Xamilpan point.
Bottom row: Tortugas point, Seda point. Scale 1.25 : 1.

FIG. 29.   Top row: Harrell point, Matamoros point.   Bottom row: Tula point, Drill.   Scale 1.25:1.

is some flaking on the ventral surface especially near the point.

Only one point of this type was found at Tamaulipas and its chronological position is not firm (MacNeish, 1958: pp. 63–74, fig. 25–1).   At Tehuacan 11 of the 13 specimens were from the Venta Salada phase (Mac-Neish and others, 1967: pp. 75–76, table 10).

Xamilpan
(fig. 28)

Total number of specimens: 3.

Material: 3 chert.

Dimensions: length: 2.7 cm.–2.8 cm.; width (maximum width is at the base): 1.5 cm.–1.7 cm.; thickness: 0.3 cm.–0.4 cm.; notch length: 0.3 cm.–0.5 cm.; notch width: 0.15 cm.–0.3 cm.

Indicated use: arrow heads.

These specimens all have straight tapering edges, a straight base, and side notches.   Irregular flaking is confined to the dorsal surface.   The ventral surface shows pressure flaking around the point.   One specimen shows basal thinning.

This type has not been reported from Tehuacan, the Valley of Mexico, or Tamaulipas.   It resembles the Teotihuacan types, but is sufficiently different in form to justify a separate designation.   It may be, however, a local variant of the Teotihuacan type.

Tortugas
(fig. 28)

Total number of specimens: 3.

Material: 3 chert.

Dimensions: (no complete specimens) length: 7.5 cm. (reconstructed), width: 2.5 cm.–3.9 cm.; thickness: 0.7 cm.–0.9 cm.

Indicated use: spear or lance heads.

These points have parallel edges to mid-length and possibly straight tapering edges from mid-length to pointed end. The base is straight. The specimens appear to have been formed by percussion flaking. The edges are retouched. All bases show marked thinning. Like the 2 Texacoco examples, the 3 fragmentary specimens have their pointed ends snapped off.

MacNeish and others (1967: p. 60) note that this type has been found in Chiapas, Puebla, Hidalgo, Tamaulipas, and Texas. They do not appear at Tehuacan after the Santa Maria phase, but are found in the Los Angeles phase at Tamaulipas (MacNeish, 1958: table 3) which is contemporary with the Tepexi phases.

Matamoros
(fig. 29)

Total number of specimens: 2.

Material: 2 chert.

Dimensions: (no complete specimens) length: 5.0 cm. (reconstructed); width: 2.5 cm.; thickness: 0.3 cm.–0.6 cm.

Indicated use: dart or spear heads.

These are stemless points with slightly convex edges and straight bases. There are irregular flake scars on both surfaces, and the edges show fine retouching. There is no basal thinning.

MacNeish and others (1967: p. 72) suggest a wide distribution from Chiapas to Texas. At Tamaulipas they appear as early as 2000 B.C., but are preponderantly in the Los Angeles phase (MacNeish, 1958: table 3). Similarly, at Tehuacan the greatest number is found in the Venta Salada phase (MacNeish and others, 1967: table 10). Both the Los Angeles phase and the Venta Salada phase are contemporary with the Tepexi phases.

Tula
(fig. 29)

Total number of specimens: 2.

Material: 2 obsidian.

Dimensions: (no complete specimens) length: 1.8 cm.–3.5 cm. (postulated); width: 1.0 cm.–1.6 cm.; thickness: 0.3 cm.–0.35 cm.

Indicated use: arrow heads.

These are stemless points made on prismatic blades. They have straight edges and bases. One specimen shows flaking on the dorsal surface, and both specimens show bifacial retouching along the edges and base.

MacNeish and others (1967: p. 76) note they are widespread in Mesoamerica in the Classic and Postclassic, but they are not found in Tamaulipas. All excavated specimens at Tehuacan were found in the Venta Salada phase (MacNeish and others, 1967: table 10).

Seda
(fig. 28)

Total number of specimens: 1.

Material: 1 chert.

Dimensions: length: 7.5 cm., width: 3.8 cm., thickness: 0.8 cm.

Indicated use: lance head.

This is a stemless point which resembles the Tortugas and Matamoros types, but not sufficiently to be classified with them. It is in the shape of an isosceles triangle with straight edges and a slightly concave base. The surface is bifurcated by short wide flake scars which reach to the center on each side. The edges and base are bifacially retouched.

Not Identified

Total number of specimens: 4.

Material: 2 obsidian, 2 chert.

These specimens could be identified as points, but were too fragmentary to be typed or described adequately.

DRILLS
(fig. 29)

Total number of specimens: 4.

Material: 1 obsidian, 3 chert.

Dimensions: (no complete specimens) length: 5.5 cm. (reconstructed); width of base: 2.5 cm. (reconstructed); width of shaft: 0.9 cm.–1.4 cm.; thickness: 0.5 cm.–0.8 cm.

Indicated use: drills.

These can be described as asymmetrical flaring-based drills. They are pointed with long, narrow, tapering shafts, and are lens-shaped or hemispheric in cross-section. The specimens show irregular flake scars on both surfaces, and have finely to roughly retouched edges. One specimen shows basal thinning.

CRUDE OVOID BIFACES
(fig. 30)

Total number of specimens: 2.

Material: 1 chert, 1 quartzite.

Dimensions: length: 7.1 cm.–8.0 cm.; width: 3.7 cm.–4.1 cm.; thickness: 1.6 cm.–1.9 cm.

These flakes show the large, rough scars of percussion flaking. The edges have been thinned on both surfaces by a series of blows around the periphery. Such bifaces are widespread in time and space in the New World and they have not been typed. These are similar to those found at Tehuacan (MacNeish and others, 1967: pp. 89–90).

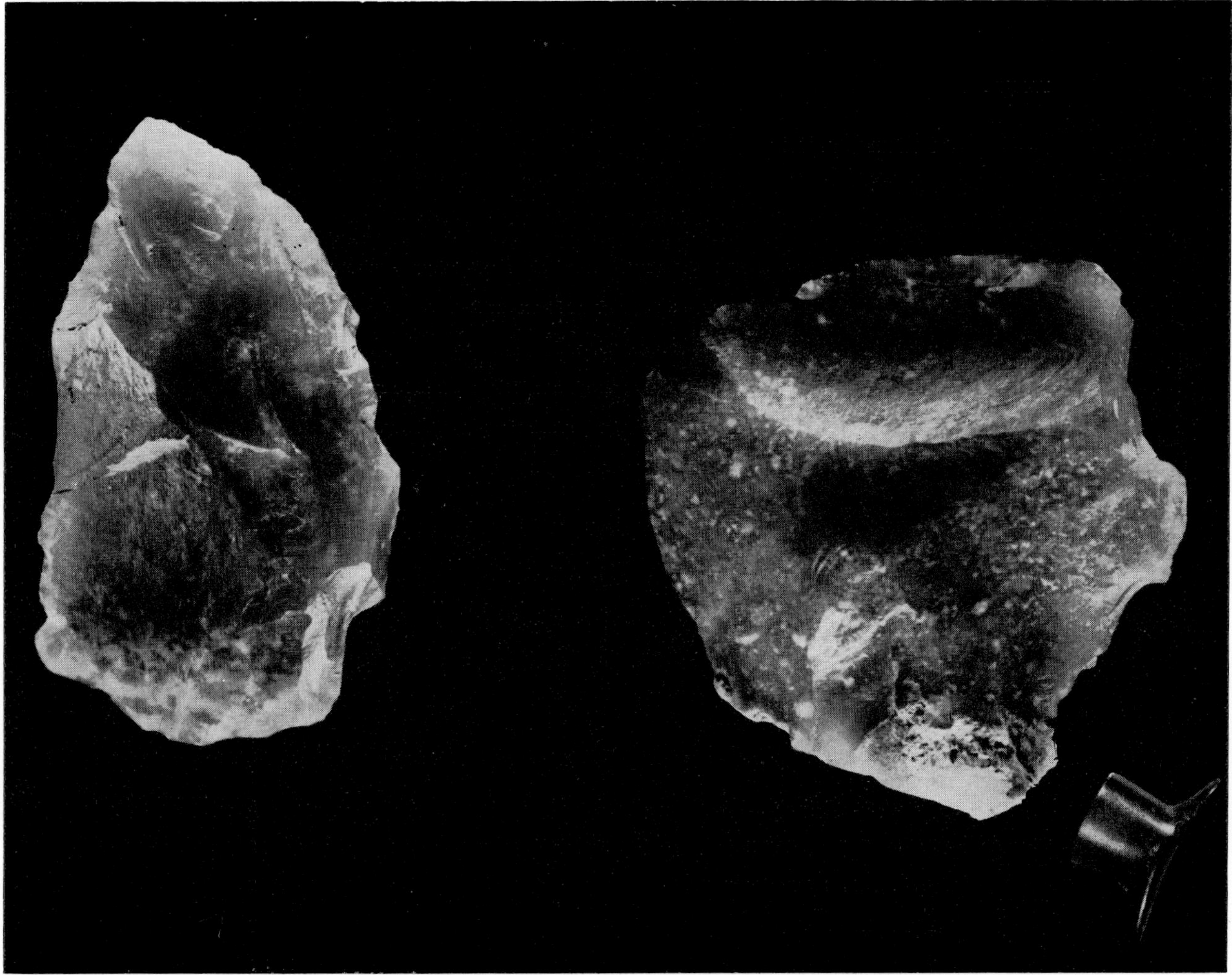

FIG. 30. Crude ovoid biface, Crude discoid biface, labret. Scale 1.25 : 1.

CRUDE DISCOID BIFACE
(fig. 30)

Total number of specimens: 1.
Material: 1 chert.
Dimensions: length: 6.2 cm.; width: 5.9 cm.; thickness: 2.3 cm.
This flake shows the rough scars of percussion flaking on both surfaces. The biface has been shaped and the edges thinned by a series of blows around the periphery. This type has been found in the early horizons at Tamaulipas and Tehuacan (MacNeish and others, 1967: p. 91).

POLISHED STONE
Labret
(fig. 30)

Total number of specimens: 1.
Material: 1 obsidian.
Dimensions: length: 1.0 cm.; stem diameter: 1.1 cm.; stem aperture: 0.4 cm.; flaring cross-bar length: 2.1 cm.; flaring cross-bar width: 1.1 cm.

This specimen has a cylindrical body and a thin flaring cross-bar. There is a small aperture in the center of the head of the body.

MacNeish and others (1967: p. 136) report three excavated specimens from Santa Maria phase levels at Tehuacan. Bernal (1948–1949: p. 43) reports one specimen from Coixtlahuaca.

Earplug

One fragment of obsidian is identified as part of the backing and stem of an earplug.

Ovoid

A fragment of basalt cannot be described formally or identified functionally.

CONCLUSION

The investigation at Tepexi el Viejo has contributed to the delineation of Mixteca-Puebla culture history

TABLE 5
STONE ARTIFACTS

FLAKES	**1198**	
TRIMMING FLAKES	913	
BLADES	287	
Fine Blades, Ground striking platform, snapped end	76	
Fine Blades, Snapped bulbar end	127	
Fine Blades, snapped ends	15	
Crude Blades, Prepared striking platform	18	
Crude Blades, Pointed striking platform	27	
Crude Blades, snapped ends	24	
CORES	**5**	
CRUDE CYLINDRICAL NUCLEI	3	
FINE BULLET SHAPED NUCLEI	2	
FACIALLY TRIMMED ARTIFACTS	**79**	
BLADE SPOKESHAVES	7	
BLADE SIDE SCRAPERS	3	
BLADE END SCRAPERS	8	
FLAKE SIDE SCRAPERS	2	
FLAKE SPOKESHAVES	5	
FLAKE GRAVERS	13	
GRAVER ON A POINT	1	
POINTS	33	
Texcoco		7
Harrell		6
Teotihuacan		5
Xamilpan		3
Tortugas		3
Matamoros		2
Tula		2
Seda		1
Not identified		4
DRILLS	4	
CRUDE OVOID BIFACES	2	
CRUDE DISCOID BIFACES	1	
POLISHED STONE	**3**	
LABRET	1	
EARPLUG	1	
OVOID	1	

and has also provided results which can aid in the understanding of the process by which military-political systems change.

CULTURAL HISTORY

Three phases have been established for Tepexi: the Huichi, the Xaqua, and the Toyna. Both pottery and architecture have been used to devise this periodization. The chronological sequence from the Valley of Mexico, based on pottery types, has been especially useful as a guide in arriving at the sequence for Tepexi (Tolstoy, 1958: pp. 63–64, 71–72).

HUICHI PHASE

The Huichi phase is marked by the arrival and settlement of the population at the site. While the entire present area of the site was apparently occupied in the Huichi phase, the major construction of the main precinct was done for the most part in the two later periods. The pottery of the Huichi phase is found at all subsites as well as in the main precinct. The variant architectural style of the structures of Subsites I and III are the same as C-Wall-2 which excavations indicated was the earliest structure of the main precinct.

No other structure in the main precinct was of this style. Excavation revealed that Sector C was built up to its final level at this time. Thus, both the pottery and the architecture show that the main precinct and the subsites were occupied during the Huichi phase and that the major constructions were built later.

In dating the Huichi phase, reliance was placed on types that have been assigned chronological positions in other regions of Mesoamerica. While there are sherds in the collection with modes that have been used as markers for the Classic period, they were not found in stratified deposits at Tepexi. Therefore, there is no reason to assign the Huichi phase a Classic date on the basis of these modes alone. In any case there are too few of these modes to suggest a Classic date. These sherds are simply regarded as of a Classic period and existing in a later period.

The presence of Huajuapan Domestic Thin Orange of the Ñuiñe style period (late Classic and early Postclassic), early Postclassic Plumbate, and Culhuacan Black/Orange in the lowest levels was evaluated more carefully. The existence of early Postclassic pottery types in levels 16 and 17 made it necessary to weigh the possibility that the beginning of Huichi should be

TABLE 6

Chronological Sequences in Mesoamerica

(years)	VALLEY OF OAXACA	MIXTECA ALTA	TEPEXI	TEHUACAN	CHOLULA	CENTRAL PLATEAU
1500						
	Monte Alban Vb		Toyna			
1400					Cholulteca III	Late Aztec
			Xaqua			
1300	Yagul Palace / Monte Alban Va	Coixtlahuaca	Puichi		Cholulteca II	
1200						Early Aztec
1100	Monte Alban IV	Nochistlan-Natividad Phase				
1000						
900	Yagul Mound 5W					Toltec-Mazapan
800					Cholulteca I	Coyotlatelco
700				Venta Salada		Teotihuacan-Metepec
600	Monte Alban IIIb					
500						Teotihuacan-Xolalpan
400						Teotihuacan-Tlamimilolpa
300		Nochistlan-Las Flores Phase				Teotihuacan-Miccaotli
200						
100	Monte Alban IIIa / Mitla South Group Built	Nochistlan-Ramos Phase			Palo Seco	Teotihuacan-Tzacualli

Tepexi column vertical label (top to bottom): Codices of the Puebla-Mixteca style — Mixtec Dynasties of the Puebla-Mixteca style — Nuiñe style dated early Postclassic, that is, around A.D. 900. However, the appraisal of two data resulted in placing the beginning of the Huichi phase at A.D. 1300. First, some earlier types always appear in later deposits. Second, the levels which contained Culhuacan Black/Orange also contained Tenochtitlan Black/Orange. While Culhuacan Black/Orange appears in the Valley of Mexico before, it continues into the Early Aztec period (A.D. 1200-A.D. 1400). Tenochtitlan Black/Orange occurs in the Early Aztec period although it reaches its peak at the beginning of the Late Aztec (A.D. 1400-contact). Thus, the placement of Huichi as beginning in A.D. 1300 seems most in harmony with all available data.

Documentary evidence indicates that in A.D. 1297 the Tolteca-Chichimeca migrants to Cholula wrested power from the resident Olmeca-Xicalanca. Considering that the pottery points to an A.D. 1300 date for the advent of the earliest phase at Tepexi and that the proportion of Cholula Polychrome at Tepexi is far greater than any other pottery with cultural affiliation elsewhere, it seems possible that Tepexi was founded by refugee Olmeca-Xicalanca. The eight ceramic groups (Almongo, Huajoyuca, Chochos, Coatepetl, Calco, Hondo, Mimiapan, and Canal) which occur in greater proportion than Cholula Polychrome appear to be local with no outside cultural affiliations. This would indicate that the refugees from Cholula incorporated the local population into the newly founded community.

Perhaps the Olmeca-Xicalanca did not originate in the Mixteca Baja-southern Puebla region as Jiménez Moreno (1966: p. 62) has suggested, but moved into the region *after* they left Cholula. This does not dispute Jiménez Moreno's contention that the Olmeca-Xicalanca were tri-ethnic, that is, Nahua, Chocho-Popoloca, and Mixtec, nor that these languages were intermingled in the Mixteca Baja-southern Puebla region in the sixteenth century. It seems more likely that the Cholula style formed within a short period of time at Cholula itself, as Jiménez Moreno (1966: p. 62) has also suggested, and the Cholula style we see at Tepexi may have been brought there by the Olmeca-Xicalanca who were moving from Cholula south and were reported in the Mixteca Baja-southern Puebla region in the sixteenth century.

Ceramic groups which appear in the Huichi phase but are represented by a small number of sherds are Yagul, Mila, Zacapala, Xochitlan, and Gracias. Groups which occur predominately in the Huichi phase are Almolongo, Chochos, Huajoyuca, and Tepexi.

Among the special wares and types Huajuapan Domestic Thin Orange, Mixtec Polychrome, Plumbate, Texcoco Moulded, and Tenochititlan Black/Orange occur exclusively in the Huichi phase. Culhuacan Black/Orange appears predominately in the Huichi. Only a small proportion appears in Xaqua levels.

Xaqua phase

The Xaqua phase is marked primarily by the building up of the remaining four artificial levels within the main precinct and the undertaking of considerable major construction there. In Sector A the outer walls, A-Wall-1, 2, 3, 4, and 5 were built as well as the pyramidal platform and mound with recess. In Sector B the outer walls B-Wall-1 and 2 and the pyramidal platform and the mound with recess were constructed. In Sector C outer walls C-Wall-1 and 3 were built as was the building complex within that sector. It was during this phase that the construction of the lower courses of D-Wall-1 and E-Wall-1, 2, and 3 was undertaken.

Thus, in the Xaqua phase the entire main precinct was surrounded by outer walls, and the five levels had been built up artificially (the Sector C level had been built up in the Huichi phase). In addition the pyramidal platforms, mounds with recesses, and the building complex in Sector C were constructed. That is, by the end of this phase all of the main precinct construction, except for the building complexes of Sectors D and E, was completed.

The Xaqua phase is dated as between A.D. 1350 and A.D. 1450. There are no data which permit a direct dating of this phase. It falls between Huichi and Toyna whose initial dates have been set at A.D. 1300 and A.D. 1450 respectively. Considering the amount of construction during this phase, it seems likely that it lasted longer than Huichi. Thus, it is assigned a period of one hundred years.

This phase is defined primarily on the basis of architectural features. However, despite some levels with sherds out of chronological order, it has been possible by separating mixed and unmixed levels to note the ceramic groups which appear predominately in the Xaqua phase. These are Calco, Hondo, Canal, Comulco, and Mimiapan. Ceramic groups which occur exclusively in the Xaqua phase, but are represented by a small number are Ayutla, Coixtlahuaca, and Xamilpan. The groups which occur in the greatest proportions in Xaqua are Coatepetl, Almolongo, Calco, Huajoyuca, and Hondo.

TOYNA PHASE

The Toyna phase is marked by the construction of the building complexes in Sectors D and E, the construction of certain walls in Sectors D, E, B, and C, and the appearance of Tlatelolco Black/Orange. This pottery type is restricted to the Late Aztec period (A.D. 1400 to Conquest), but it seems to occur in some areas around A.D. 1500 only. Since the stratigraphic evidence indicates that the building complexes of Sectors D and E were built sometime before the introduction of Tlatelolco Black/Orange, the beginning of the Toyna phase is dated at A.D. 1450.

The pottery represented in the greatest proportions in the Toyna phase is Coatepetl, Ixcaquistla, Almolongo, and Chochos groups, Cholula Polychrome ware, and Huajoyuca and Xolochta groups. Of the groups Coatepetl and Ixcaquistla occur predominately in the Toyna phase, and Ixcaquistla occurs predominately in this phase in a number large enough for the chi-square test to be applicable. Balsas, Rosario, and Xolochta groups also occur exclusively in the Toyna phase, but in a small number.

The construction of the new building complexes required additions to existing walls. Upper courses were added to D-Wall-1. The style of these courses is one assigned to the Xaqua phase. But since these walls were made higher to accommodate the building complexes of the Toyna phase, it is presumed they were built in either late Xaqua or early Toyna.

The upper courses of E-Wall-1, 2, and 3 are of the same style as the architecture of the building complexes, and were assigned to the Toyna phase. In addition, new walls were built. B-Wall-3 was built between Sector B and the new Sector D, and B-Wall-4 was constructed setting Sector E apart from Sector B. D-Wall-2 separated Sector D from Sector E. The construction of the new building complexes, then, did not require enlarging the site, rather it was based upon the demarcation of new sectors within the main precinct and the building up of already existing walls.

Other building programs seem to have been undertaken as well. B-Wall-5 was built. Its 5-meter height definitively separates Sector B and Sector A (unlike the rest of the boundary wall between the two sectors which was probably about 1 meter high). The subsector in Sector A was created by B-Wall-5 together with the older A-Wall-1 and 2.

Some rebuilding seems to have taken place also. B-Wall-6 was built at this time and seems to have replaced F-Wall-1. C-Wall-4 was built, perhaps to cover the otherwise unprotected northeast section of the building complex in Sector C.

The date of A.D. 1450 which marks the beginning of the Toyna phase is reinforced by the documentary evidence which indicates that around A.D. 1438 Tlatelolco was making forays into Puebla, and sealing political alliances by marriage with local noble families. Such a marriage was arranged between a noblewoman of Tlatelolco and a nobleman of Tepexi. It may be that we are seeing the Tlatelolco influence in the construction of the new building complexes.

In any case, the residences of the nobles appear to have either expanded or shifted from the subsites to the main precinct in the Toyna phase. The new building complexes had two characteristics the older complexes lacked. First, they encompassed a larger area, and second, they were within the protection of the fortified main precinct. From this we may conclude that the nobility was expanding and that greater attention was being accorded their security. It is hard to determine whether this more intense concern was due to an accelerated pace of military attacks on Tepexi, or to an advance in military strategy.

It was during the Toyna phase that Tepexi was conquered by the Mexicans (A.D. 1503). Excavation does not indicate that Tepexi was razed or abandoned at this time as has been suggested by Carmen Cook de Leonard (1961: p. 91). Indeed, this would seem unlikely considering the known Mexican pattern of conquest. Towns were not destroyed because they were conquered for the tribute they could provide. Nor was the population forced to move to make way for Mexicans. There were no Mexican occupations of towns. After conquest towns remained as before except that they were poorer by the goods and products sent to the Valley of Mexico.

TEPEXI AFTER CONQUEST

In A.D. 1520 Cortés, with the help of the Tlaxcallans, conquered Tepexi el Viejo. Some time between A.D. 1520 and A.D. 1537 the inhabitants of Tepexi el Viejo moved southeast to the site of the present Tepexi de Rodríguez. Undoubtedly, the war casualties, the famine, and the smallpox epidemics between A.D. 1519 and A.D. 1524 reduced the population. The Spaniards, nevertheless, demanded the same tribute of Tepexi as had the Mexicans. The encroaching erosion and the decimated population made it increasingly difficult to reap from the land its previous yields. In addition, many of the political functions of the town were fast following the military into obsolescence.

While the Spaniards vitiated the old system, they also brought elements which could be used in building a new one. It was the silk industry established in A.D. 1537 at the site of Tepexi de Rodríguez which accounts for Tepexi's continuity as a community from prehistoric into historic times.

CULTURAL AFFILIATIONS

The explication of cultural history not only requires the delineation of cultural events through time, but also cultural connections through space. Tepexi, like Cholula, has been placed in a no-man's land between the Central Mexican region and the Mixteca or Oaxaca region. Sometimes, inexplicably, included in the former and never in the latter. The examination of its cultural affiliations revealed through this investigation has led to the placement of Tepexi within an archaeological spatial unit and has helped define that unit.

It is significant that Cholula Polychrome occurs at a higher percentage than any other decorated ware throughout the history of Tepexi. It has been suggested here that this may be because Tepexi was founded by the Olmeca-Xicalanca after they left Cholula. If this is true, they apparently continued their ties with that center. In any case the pottery analysis indicates Tepexi had close connection with Cholula from Huichi through Toyna times. (Ironically, this ancient association has been maintained in modern times by pot hunters who have potted Tepexi for Cholula Polychrome which they have brought to Cholula to sell.)

The modes which point to a relationship between Cholula and Tepexi are the painted dotted circle motif, painting in more than three colors, decorative field entirely covered with motifs in an interlocking pattern, painted spiral and step motif in combination, conical support, painted undulating lines paralleling rim, painted rim band, painted spiral motif, cross-cutting horizontal and vertical parallel lines with circles, crenelated slab support, painted step-fret, and zoomorphic support.

One problem concerning Tepexi's relations with Cholula has not been resolved. The division of Cholula Polychrome into *policroma laca, mate,* and *firme* at Cholula (Noguera, 1954) does not exist in that chronological order at Tepexi. The reasons for this are not fully understood. It may be that the existence of both *policroma laca* and *policroma firme* on all levels indicates that Tepexi's lowest levels are contemporaneous with Cholulteca III, and that *policroma laca* is an example of an earlier type in use at a later period. If that is true, all the phases at Tepexi would be contemporaneous with Cholulteca III. To place the three Tepexi phases in that period would require an interpretation of the Valley of Mexico pottery types in the Tepexi strata which would be forced and unrealistic, namely, that all the Early Aztec sherds were remanent, and that the entire history of Tepexi was less than one hundred years. Since work is now being done at Cholula and the Cholulteca sequence may be revised, the sequence was not used as a chronological guide.

The architecture at Tepexi does not specifically resemble the styles at Cholula. As will be seen, the Tepexi architectural style is believed to have other connections.

While affiliations with the Valley of Oaxaca, the Mixteca Alta, the Mixteca Baja, and Puebla are clear, since the Postclassic sequences for these regions have not been detailed, it is possible to make only the most general alignments.

In the Valley of Oaxaca, Bernal's (1966a: p. 365) investigations at Yagul, Mitla, Monte Albán, Cuilapan, and Zaachila have led him to propose two subphases for Monte Albán V. The A.D. 1250 to A.D. 1450 dates for Monte Albán Va make it approximately coeval with Huichi and Xaqua, while Monte Albán Vb dated at about A.D. 1450 is contemporary with the Toyna phase at Tepexi.

There are indications of cultural continuity between Monte Albán Va and Vb, but the second phase seems to have been a time of population expansion. This is parallel to events at Tepexi at about the same time.

Unlike Tepexi, however, polychrome pottery comes into the Valley in Monte Albán Vb. At Tepexi polychrome pottery is found in the earliest phase.

The Fine Gray Ware at Tepexi appears similar to fine gray ware at Yagul and the Ocotlan Graphite similar to the graphite on red noted for Yagul and Zaachila. The modes which point to an affiliation with the Valley of Oaxaca are painting in more than three colors, decorative field entirely covered with motifs in an interlocking pattern, painted spiral and step motif, conical support finger impressions in the clay, painted spiral motif crenelated slab support, use of graphite for decoration, zoomorphic support, and high straight neck.

The Mixteca Alta is not very well known archaeologically. Bernal (1948–1949: pp. 70–76) offers a tentative chronology for Coixtlahuaca. The absence of Tenayuca Black/Orange (Aztec II) and the presence of Tenochtitlan Black/Orange (Aztec III) suggests to him a late Postclassic date for the site. This would make it contemporary with Tepexi. The polished gray ware found at all levels at Coixtlahuaca is also found at all levels at Tepexi (Coixtlahuaca Ceramic Group). The Fine Gray Ware at Tepexi also has parallels at Coixtlahuaca.

Spores (1969: pp. 561–563) has designated a Natividad phase dating from around A.D. 1000 to the Conquest. He has also pointed out that pottery design elements which appear in the Natividad phase have been noted at Tehuacan (Venta Salada Phase) and at Cholula. These combinations of dots, circles, and geometric forms have been found at Tepexi in all phases. Other modes which link Tepexi with the Mixteca Alta are the straight slab support, painting in more than three colors, painted straight lines paralleling rim, painted rim band, lustrous black or dark gray slip, silty texture, painted short parallel vertical lines, molded geometric motifs on vessel floor and lower inner wall, crenelated slab support, and the use of graphite for decoration.

The entire sequence at Tepexi fits within the Tehuacan Venta Salada phase, which is dated A.D. 700/800—Conquest. Since the Venta Salada phase has not been broken down into smaller units further alignment is not possible.

The full report on the pottery at Tehuacan has not been published at this writing, and so it is not possible to compare the pottery with any degree of completeness. However, a comparison of the Tepexi and Tehuacan collections reveal that the Molcaxac, Mila and Tepeaca Ceramic Groups were present in the Venta Salada phase at Tehuacan. Also found in both Venta Salada phase, Tehuacan and Tepexi pottery were the following modes: incised line or lines parallel to rim, painted lines paralleling rim, lustrous black or dark gray slip, crenelated slab support, painted undulating lines diagonal to rim, painted fret, zoomorphic support, and motifs found in the Codex Borgia. It has been suggested

(Chadwick and MacNeish, 1967: pp. 114–115) that these motifs may occur exclusively in the general region of the Señorío de Teotitlan. They do, however, occur at Tepexi, Itzocan, Molcaxac and Acatlan.

The stone artifacts compare closely with the Venta Salada phase artifacts on the whole. A notable difference is that crude blades and crude cylindrical nuclei are in far greater proportion at Tepexi than in the Venta Salada phase. At Tehuacan they occur with greater frequency in earlier phases.

The study of the pottery from other sites in the Puebla region indicates that Thin Slip Gray-Black and Red-Yellow Wares and El Zapote and Comulco Ceramic groups may be among the distinctive pottery for the region in the late Postclassic.

The modes linking sites in that region are straight slab support, painted dotted circle motif, decorative motifs resembling elements in the Codex Borgia, incised line or lines parallel to rim, griddle with ridged rim, nubbin appendage, base with rounded obtuse angle, painted undulating lines paralleling rim, painted spiral motif, silty texture, molded geometric motifs on vessel floor and lower inner walls.

Tepexi's affiliation with the Mixteca Baja is manifested in the modes associated with Acatlan Polychrome and Huajuapan Domestic Thin Orange. Since there are almost no collections from the Baja available for comparison, very little more can be said. However, this does not mean that Tepexi's ties with the Mixteca Baja were weak. The historical record indicates that Tepexi's association with the Baja may have been stronger than with the Alta or Puebla. More archaeological work needs to be done in the Baja in order to determine the nature of the relationship that is sketched in the documentary sources.

Beyond the Mixteca-Puebla regions the important affiliations seem to be with the Valley of Mexico and Veracruz. The association with the Valley of Mexico is seen in the earliest period and continued throughout Tepexi's history. This is indicated by the Red Ware and the painted Orange Ware from the Valley of Mexico. Since there was no increase in Orange Ware after the Mexican conquest, it does not appear that Tepexi was occupied by the Mexicans, and the presence of Tlatelolco Black/Orange indicates that it was not abandoned at that time.

The distinctive mode of a lustrous white surface is found in the unclassified polychromes at Tepexi and in pottery from Tlanhualpa, Tuxpilla, Tihuatlan, and Tabuco as well as Totonacapan. Jiménez Moreno (1966: p. 14) has noted trails from Tepexi to Tehuacan, and, from there, on to El Trapiche in the region of Cempoala, and another to La Mixtequilla and Los Tuxtlas near Cerro de Las Mesas and Tres Zapotes. The purposes these routes served need to be investigated.

The architectural style at Tepexi contributes few data on the question of affiliation within the Mixteca-Puebla region but does permit the formulation of some hypotheses. The construction of walls at the site of Santo Domingo in the Cañada region of Oaxaca (Bernal, 1966b) bears a close resemblance to the earliest rough style variant at Tepexi. Bernal points out the similarities between the architecture of Santo Domingo and that of Yagul, Mitla, and Matatlan and suggests that the "eastern Mixtecs" of the Valley of Oaxaca may have their antecedents in this region which is on the eastern border of the Mixteca Alta. This is in harmony with Jiménez Moreno's (1966: p. 61) suggestion, made on the basis of historic data, that "the cradle of the dynasties that ruled the Mixtecs" was situated in this region.

Almost nothing is known about the architectural style of the Mixteca Alta. Certainly the method of using small stones between large blocks used in the construction of walls at Coixtlahuaca was not employed at Tepexi. There are resemblances in the piling of building blocks inside mounds at Tilantongo and Tepexi, but they hardly indicate a definitive connection. Single traits at Tepexi such as the use of blocks of caliche in wall construction are found at Quiotepec, not too far from Santo Domingo (Pareyón Moreno, 1960: p. 99), and at a number of sites in the Mixteca Alta, including Yatachío (Paddock, 1953: p. 12; 1966: p. 182). The use of pulverized caliche in flooring is also found in southern Puebla sites such as Ixcaquistla, Metzontla, and San Luis Temalacayuca, and a site near Huajuapan in the Mixteca Baja (Cook de Leonard, 1953: p. 435; Paddock, 1966: p. 182).

Similarity in architectural style is very often concealed by the construction material used and by the varying functions of the structures. For example, the same type of wall construction may have an entirely different appearance built in caliche from what it would have if it were built in adobe. In the same way, function may have a determinative hold on construction. The attempt to build structures designed specifically for different functions can produce what seems to be different styles.

What we may have in the Mixteca-Puebla region is an architectural style that began on the eastern borders of the Mixteca Alta and moved west where different materials and varying functions altered its appearance, and only a few scattered traits testify to its coherence.

The Tepexi style is very likely a local manifestation of this widespread style. It is in the presence of Cholula Polychrome along with local wares and ceramic groups and along with the generalized Mixteca-Puebla architectural style which we see in the Huichi phase that points to the amalgamation of the Olmeca-Xicalanca and the local population in the founding of Tepexi.

The Tepexi investigation points both to the coherence of the Mixteca-Puebla region as a valid archaeological spatial unit and to the distinctiveness of the Puebla subregion within that unit. There seems to be no justification for putting this subregion in Central Mexico. It also suggests that the connections between the Puebla subregion and the Mixteca Baja after A.D. 1300 may be stronger than has been recognized and merits further investigation.

CULTURAL CHANGE

The conclusions concerning the process of change in the military-political system in the Postclassic is based on an evaluation of the archaeological data which relate most closely to the way a community has used the landscape to maintain itself as a socio-cultural entity. For this discussion it is necessary to distinguish between the spatial units settlement, zone, and territory, and the societal unit community. A settlement refers to habitations, public structures, and features which are utilized, such as land, rivers, and rock outcrops, whose spatial relationships can be plotted on a map. These habitations, public structures, and features are employed by members of a community who have a continuous and personal relationship. A zone refers to settlements, usually contiguous, with all or some of these characteristics whose members form a wider community based on social and/or political relationships involving some, but not continual, personal connection. A territory refers to zones (though sometimes settlements as well), not always contiguous, whose members form an even wider community based on political relationships, primarily, and involving little personal association. The spatial differential between a territory and a zone is much greater than that between the settlement and the zone. Since settlement, zone, and territory are spatial units, and community is a social unit, there are settlement communities, zonal communities, and territorial communities.

Four characteristics have been used in ranging communities along a continuum of development: permanence, nucleation, population size and density, and chorism. Tepexi was a permanent, nucleated settlement. The main precinct and the three contiguous subsites (Subsites I, II, and III) were functionally part of a single ceremonial, civic, commercial, and residential unit. The entire settlement area, including the nucleated and more dispersed area of occupation but excluding the settlement lands, was estimated to be approximately 2.5 square kilometers. The lands of the settlement were the narrow cultivable Xamilpan Valley, the southern extension of the Tepexi hill, and the hills to the northeast and southwest.

Since there were no satisfactory documentary sources, an attempt was made to arrive at a population estimate on the basis of dwelling area, that is, actual living or roofed-over floor space. Raoul Naroll (1962) has written on the allometric relation between settlement population and floor area, that is, the linear relation between the logs of these quantities. He computes a regression of the form $F = aP^b$ where F is the roofed-over floor area in thousands of square meters and P is settlement population in thousands. He presents data for the largest settlement of eighteen societies, mostly from North America and Oceania, but he includes some from South America, Africa, and Eurasia, and computes a regression equation $\log F = \log a + b \log P$. Because of an apparent misprint in the Naroll article this regression was recomputed using Smillie's (1969) STATPACKI in the APL programming language. The formula from this recomputation used here to estimate the population was $F = 7.2896\, P^{\,0.842646}$. He also suggests that the population can be estimated roughly as 1/10 the roofed-over floor area in square meters since, by eye, this straight line seems to fit the logs of the data almost as well as the regression line.

In order to estimate the population at Tepexi it was first necessary to determine the roofed-over floor area. The building complexes of the main precinct constituted the roofed-over floor area. They covered 2,556 square meters out of a total of 18,750 square meters for the whole main precinct. Three subsites (I, II, and III) were considered to be intensively occupied on the basis of the density of artifacts on the surface and remanent walls and structures. The area of all three subsites was calculated to be a total of about 119,500 square meters. Since some of this area was occupied with non-residential structures, plazas, alleyways, and so on, only half of the 119,500 square meters was considered to be roofed-over floor space, that is, 59,750 square meters were calculated to be the subsite roofed-over floor space. Thus, a total of 62,306 square meters (2,556 square meters for the main precinct plus 59,750 square meters for the subsites) was calculated as the roofed-over floor area for the settlement. Using the recomputed Naroll formula the result was a population estimate of slightly more than 12,500 for Tepexi based on 62,000 square meters of roofed-over floor space. Using 1/10 the roofed-over floor area in square meters to estimate the population, the result was about 6,000, that is, 1/10 of 62,000. While neither of these methods is fully satisfactory, the resultant population estimates of 6,000 and 12,500 are not incompatible Postconquest information on Tepexi. In 1565 the population of Tepexi was recorded as between 10,000 and 11,000 (Cook and Simpson, 1949: pp. 70–71).

Since the area of the entire settlement was 2.5 square kilometers, a population of 6,000 would yield a population density of 2,400 per square kilometer, and a population of 12,500 would yield a population density of 5,000 per square kilometer. In either case the population size and density would make Tepexi comparable to settlements elsewhere in Mesoamerica which have been considered towns or small cities (*cf.* Sanders and Price, 1968: pp. 47, 151).

Tepexi was synchoritic. The tribute record indicates that Tepexi was the center of a zonal community, that is, it had subject hamlets. Some of these appear to have been in the immediately adjacent *Tierra Caliente*. The zonal community seems to have been well integrated in the Mixteca Alta (Spores, 1967: p. 103), and the unity with which it is described in the tribute record indicates that it was probably well-integrated at Tepexi. The political and economic demands made by the center on the population of the zone appear to have been the same as those made on the population of the settlement.

Beyond the zone was the tributary territory. The territory was unbounded in any strict sense, but it is clearly defined in the sources as lying between Tepexi and Piaxtla, Acatlan, Petlalcingo, Chazumbá and Zapotitlán (Cuthá) to the south and Huatlatlauca to the north. Wars were fought between Tepexi and these centers over the tributary communities that were situated between them. Victory meant a center could demand tribute, but it had no "legitimate" rights over these communities as it did over those in the zone. The tributary communities of the territory were politically independent and their internal affairs were their own.

Thus, Tepexi can be described as a town or small city with a zone of political and economic influence. Within this zone tribute was paid as a matter of right to the lord and was not given because of the outcome of war. In addition Tepexi was engaged in conquest within a larger area. Tributary communities won in warfare were not integrated. In the territory political connections with the center were tenuous.

The military aspect of Tepexi was oriented towards the settlement community. The main precinct contained most of the major buildings and was enclosed by great walls. They served two purposes. First, they prevented the diminution of the surface area by erosion. If these buildings had been scattered, separate walls would have been necessary for each structure. Thus, the concentration of buildings within the main precinct decreased the area where fixed boundaries had to be preserved, and the settlement community was able to maintain the sites of these buildings with a smaller amount of effort. Second, the walls were part of the fortification of the precinct. The precinct was placed on a hill that had natural military features for both defense and counterattack, and the walls enhanced these features. Militarily, it was economical to enclose only a portion of the site in order to shorten the perimeter of the defended area. An extended perimeter forces the defenders to cover a long line and prevents them from rallying quickly at the point of attack when the main assault comes. The perimeter was shortened

by building structures in a small area, and, probably, by gathering in the population at the time of battle.

Not only did the outer walls provide protection for the defenders, but they also hindered the assault, mobility, and fire-power of the attackers. An enemy assault by scaling the walls was impeded by their great height, by the lack of slope, and by the smooth plaster face without footholes.

Direct penetration, used in the attack of many town and city walls, was impossible at Tepexi since the walls were built against the hillslopes. Similarly the well-known technique of penetration from below, that is, by tunneling. could not be used since the surface of the ground inside the walls was far above the surface of the ground outside the walls.

A siege of Tepexi may have been attempted. Water storage units were not found there, but it seems likely that they would be located by more extensive excavation. It does not seem possible that no provision was made for storage. For without it, siege would have been an easy route to victory.

The defenders' first task was to prevent the enemy from storming the walls. This meant they had to maintain their fire and be protected at the same time. Where troops fight behind walls, there are, often, embrasures or crenels which enable the defender to fire while standing behind the wall. These did not exist at Tepexi. Without apertures the walls would be a hindrance if they were built higher than one meter on the inside. At Tepexi the walls which were not part of the building complexes were always less than one meter high, and usually almost even with the ground surface. The bowmen were not exposed, however, because, to judge from documentary sources, they fired from a prone position (*Historia Tolteca-Chichimeca*, 1947: lamina XXIV), and, thus, offered only a small target to the enemy. Some building complex walls seem to have had apertures. The position of one is less than 0.6 meter above ground level, and could have been used only by a man in a prone position.

The weakest points in fortifications are the gates which become places of concentrated attack and defense. The gate is commonly placed so that the attacker must place the right or unshielded side of his body towards the defenders. At Tepexi the gates were placed so as to force the enemy to attack in this way. The constructions in the southern part of Sector C may be related to the important defense of the gates. There were two gates at Tepexi. The westernmost gate was a false one and led outside the main walls. If the enemy gained access to the gate east of this one, he found himself between C-Wall-1 and F-Wall-1, hampered in his movements, and an easy target for those on both walls.

If the initial attack were successful and the attackers passed through an opening in C-Wall-1 into Sector C, the defenders were able to draw back to the inner sectors that had independent systems of defense. These sectors had their own walls and were on levels higher than the outer sectors, permitting the defenders to fire from an advantageous position on those who had gained access to the sectors below them.

The most striking architectural feature of Tepexi is its location on a hilltop. Both Torquemada (1723: p. 32) and Burgoa (1934: pp. 274–276) recount legends of the origin of the Mixtecs which refer to their early occupation of hilltops, and this pattern is found throughout the Mixteca-Puebla region. What we do not fully understand as yet is the function of the hilltop in the settlement pattern of the region. Mountains and hills were considered sacred by the Mixtecs, and it has been suggested that it was for this reason that ceremonial precincts were built there. But the work at Tepexi indicates that a reevaluation of hilltop sites in the Mixteca-Puebla region may reveal that more of the settlement than just the ceremonial structures was built on hills, and that these hills served as fortifications.

The full report on the Palo Blanco hilltop centers and the centers of the Venta Salada complex at Tehuacan should add important data. More work needs to be done also at hilltop sites in the Mixteca Alta, such as Yucuñudahui, Yucita, Cerro Encatado, Huamelulpan, Pueblo Viejo near Yatachío, Teposolula, and Mogote del Cacique. In addition, further investigations of hilltop sites in Puebla, such as Atenayuca, Cuthá, and Cerro Colorado which have been described as fortresses, and the so-called fortresses of Mitla and Yagul may reveal that they are not simply fortified points, but fortified centers or precincts. The need for protection may have become the critical factor in choosing the site of several components of the settlement. Until hilltop sites are investigated we cannot assume they are unfortified, that they are the sites of ceremonial structures alone, or that they are fortified points without non-military structures.

The political aspect of the Tepexi community can be described as having the qualities of the state. That is, there was a concentration of power in institutions which were not established solely on the basis of kinship, and force was used on behalf of those institutions to maintain that power. The expression of these qualities vary in complex societies. Concentration of political power must be evaluated in terms of the political system's relationship with other political systems, and force must be examined in terms of the nature of its expression.

The evidence indicates that its political relationship with its zone was marked by integration. Sanders (1956: pp. 126–127) has called this the "town or city state" in contrast to the "tributary empire" (Sanders, 1965: p. 73). Its political relationship with its tributary territory, however, was characterized by political decentralization rather than centralization. Tribute was collected from outlying settlements, but almost all socio-political functions seem to have been in the hands of the tributaries. In other words, political power seems to have been apportioned among Tepexi and the tributaries in its territory, perhaps not equally, but it was far from exclusively in Tepexi's hands.

What the work at Tepexi suggests is that the degree of political centralization in a tributary territory is tied to another variable. That variable is military specialization. While the ability of a state to gain and maintain a tributary territory may depend upon a low degree of military specialization, the capacity for centralizing political power seems to require a higher degree of military specialization.

At Tepexi there was a military system that was far more non-specialized than specialized. The structure of the army showed very little specialization. It is clear from the documentary sources that social leaders served military functions, and there were no specialized military leaders although there was some tactical specialization in the field. Nor was there a professional army, but simply men of the *barrios* called up for each foray, whether offensive or defensive. Troops were used for short-term actions, either to defend their own settlement or to attack another. Such limited action could be managed by a militia with ease.

No structures at Tepexi were specialized for military purposes. However, certain structures had *features* which were specialized. The profile of the walls, the series of rising levels, the positioning of the gateways served to defend the settlement by counteracting particular field tactics, and also permitted successful counterattacking.

But it was the settlement that was the focus of all military action. The fortifications protected the settlement (the public buildings, the noble residences, and as many of the rest of the population as could gather at the time of attack). Battles are recorded as being fought at the centers themselves, and tributaries changed hands on the basis of the outcome there.

The military system was not designed to relate to the tributary territory. Tepexi did not stand at a strategic point with respect to the territory. Its position on the Xamilpan River assured its water supply, but it was not strategically advantageous. The river was not a highway to its own territory, its lands, or other resources. And it was not effectively located for launching offensive action into other tributary territories. Nor is there any indication archaeologically or from documentary sources of any other fortifications of the territory, for example, at passes, or garrisons at borders. Battles are not reported to have been fought in the open territory between centers, or at the tributary settlements themselves.

In sum, Tepexi must be considered to have had a fairly non-specialized military system. There were no specialized military constructions, but some specialization of structure features, and there was little specialization in military personnel. This low degree of military specialization hindered the development of strategy and tactics in relation to the territory. The community of

Tepexi was prepared strategically and tactically to defend the settlement and to attack other center settlements, but it was not prepared for defensive and offensive action in the territory.

The investigation of Tepexi reveals a small state with a tributary territory whose political relationship with its tributaries was far more decentralized than centralized, and whose military system was more non-specialized than specialized, especially in relation to the territory. Further, it offers the hypothesis that this may have been the pattern throughout the Mixteca-Puebla region. It would appear that Mixteca-Puebla centers were also states with decentralized political systems which were limited by their military systems from achieving a high degree of political centralization.

As to more general conclusion, it would seem from this study that military specialization is not a precondition for the existence of the state with a low degree of political centralization. This observation is in harmony with Fried's (1967: pp. 104–106, 182) view based on non-archaeological data. He notes that in the evolution of political society the emergence of the state appears not to be dependent on the prior evolution of military organization or command, but on technology, economic organization, and non-military aspects of social organization. Indeed, he points out that military leaders are drawn from those with leading positions in society in general, not, as has been suggested frequently, the reverse.

This study suggests that the process of change of military-political systems may be one in which military specialization is an antecedent of political centralization. The critical aspects of military specialization necessary for political centralization seem to be the development of strategy and tactics in relation to the tributary territory, and this is dependent upon a permanent army which can be sent out to occupy the zone in long-term actions and structures which are built specifically to launch offensive and defensive action from strategic points in relation to a territory. The lack of military specialization seems to hinder, if not prevent, political centralization.

Much of the Mixteca-Puebla region was conquered by the Aztecs. That is, center by center with its tributary territory fell to the Aztecs during the fifteenth and sixteenth centuries. The Aztecs themselves, as well as a number of so-called independent kingdoms, were never drawn into any other tributary territory. This differential success indicates a change in the direction the military-political systems of the Aztec and independent kingdoms. Successful systems are perpetuated; unsuccessful systems are not.

Two hypotheses which can be offered now for testing are: that there was a higher degree of military specialization and a higher degree of political centralization in these kingdoms than in others, such as the Mixteca-Puebla, and that the higher degree of military specialization was a necessary condition for the development of a higher degree of political centralization. Indeed, what we know of the Aztecs shows them having established garrison points on territory borders and developing groups of professional warriors. They also seem to have been in flux politically, moving towards the political incorporation of the tributary territory and centralization of political power. For example, Aztec tribute collectors were beginning to seize local political authority on behalf of the Aztec state (Calnek, 1966).

The civilizations of Mesoamerica had not only differences in cultural content, that is, art, architecture, languages and so on, but also were different in the organization of society. Our recognition of these differences can help us understand the kind of changes that complex society undergoes as it evolves.

SUMMARY

This study of Tepexi el Viejo in the Mixteca-Puebla region of Mexico has traced its cultural history and has examined its military-political organization in the context of changing patterns within Mesoamerica. The settlement was occupied from about A.D. 1300 until Conquest. Perhaps it was founded by the Olmeca-Xicalanca after they were driven out of Cholula and moved south. Three phases have been defined on the basis of the analysis of architecture and pottery. They are the Huichi, from A.D. 1300 to A.D. 1350, when the subsite structures and a few structures in the main precinct were built; the Xaqua, from A.D. 1350 to A.D. 1450, when the major constructions of the main precinct were undertaken; and the Toyna, from A.D. 1450 to Conquest, when the building complexes (the noble residences) were added possibly as a result of the alliance with Tlatelolco and the expansion of the noble class. It was during this phase that Tepexi was conquered by the Mexicans in A.D. 1503 and then by Cortés in A.D. 1520. The settlement was abandoned between A.D. 1520 and A.D. 1537.

Tepexi el Viejo was a fortified settlement with a zone of political and economic influence and a tributary territory. While its zone formed a well-integrated community, its territorial community was not centralized politically, but power was diffused among the tributary settlements. Its military system was not highly specialized in personnel, equipment, or structures. It is suggested that political centralization is dependent upon military specialization and that those Mesoamerican civilizations such as the Aztec who had greater military specialization were thus able to achieve greater political centralization. Those civilizations such as the Mixtec which were not highly specialized militarily were more politically decentralized. Finally, it would seem that the direction of change in Mesoamerican civilizations was from a non-specialized military system and political decentralization to a specialized military system and political centralization.

BIBLIOGRAPHY

Anales de Tlatelolco. 1948. Fuentes para la historia de México. S. Toscano, ed. (Mexico).

ARMILLAS, PEDRO. 1951. "Mesoamerican Fortification." *Antiquity* **98**: pp. 77–86.

BARLOW, ROBERT. 1949. "The Extent of the Empire of the Culhua Mexica." *Ibero-Americana* **28**.

BERNAL, IGNACIO. 1948–1949. "Exploraciones en Coixtlahuaca." *Revista Mexicana de Estudios Antropológicos* **10**: pp. 5–76.

—— 1949. "Distribución geográfica de las culturas de Monte Albán." *El México Antiguo* **7**: pp. 209-216.

—— 1953. "Excavations in the Mixteca Alta." *Mesoamerican Notes* **3**.

—— 1958. "Archaeology of the Mixteca." *Boletín de Estudios Oaxaqueños* **7**: pp. 1–12.

—— 1965. "Archaeological Synthesis of Oaxaca." *Handbook of Middle American Indians,* R. Wauchope and G. Willey, eds. (8 v. to date, Austin) **3**, 2: pp. 788–813.

—— 1966a. "The Mixtecs in Valley Archaeology." *Ancient Oaxaca,* J. Paddock, ed. (Stanford), pp. 345–366.

—— 1966b. "Ruinas de Santo Domingo Oaxaca." *Boletín del Instituto Nacional de Antropología e Historia* **24**: pp. 8–12.

BORAH, WOODROW. 1943. *"Silk Raising in Colonial Mexico." Ibero-Americana* **20**.

BORAH, WOODROW, and SHERBURNE F. COOK. 1963. "The Aboriginal Population of Central Mexico on the Eve of the Spanish Conquest." *Ibero-Americana* **45**.

BURGOA, FRAY FRANCISCO DE. 1934. *Geográfica descripción* (2 v., Mexico).

BYERS, DOUGLAS S. 1967a. "Climate and Hydrology." *The Prehistory of the Tehuacan Valley,* D. S. Byers, ed. (2 v. to date, Austin) **1**: pp. 48–65.

—— 1967b. *The Prehistory of the Tehuacan Valley* (2 v. to date, Austin).

CALNEK, EDWARD E. 1966. "The Aztec Imperial Bureaucracy." Read at the 65th annual meeting of the American Anthropological Association, Pittsburgh.

CARREÑO, A. DE LA O. 1951. "Las provincias geohidrológicas de México." *Boletín del Instituto Geológico del Universidad Nacional Autónoma de México* **56**.

CASO, ALFONSO. 1927. "Las ruinas de Tizantlan, Tlaxcala." *Revista Mexicana de Estudios Historicos* **1**, 4: pp. 139–172.

—— 1938. "La tumba 7 de Monte Albán es mixteca." *Universidad de México* **4**, 20: pp. 117-150.

—— 1942. "Resumen del informe de las exploraciones en Oaxaca, durante la 7a y la 8a temporadas 1937–38 y 1938–39." *Actas XXVII Congreso Internacional de Americanistas, México 1939* **2**: pp. 159–187.

—— 1949. El Mapa de Teozacoalco." *Cuadernos Americanos* **8**, 5: pp. 3–40.

—— 1960a. *Interpretation of the Codex Bodley 2858* (Mexico).

—— 1960b. "Valor histórico de las codices mixtecas." *Cuadernos Americanos* **19**, 2: pp. 139–147.

—— 1962. "The Mixtec and Zapotec Cultures: The Mixtec." *Boletín de Estudios Oaxaqueños* **22**.

—— 1964. *Interpretation of the Codex Selden 3135 (A2)* (Mexico).

—— 1965. "Lapidary Work, Goldwork, and Copperwork from Oaxaca." *Handbook of Middle American Indians,* R. Wauchope and G. Willey, eds. (8 v. to date, Austin) **3**, 2: pp. 896–930.

—— 1966. "The Lords of Yanhuitlan." *Ancient Oaxaca* J. Paddock, ed. (Stanford), pp. 313-335.

CASO, ALFONSO, and JORGE ACOSTA. 1967. *La Cerámica de Monte Albán.* Memorias del Instituto Nacional de Antropología e Historia **8** (Mexico).

CASO, ALFONSO, and IGNACIO BERNAL. 1952. *Urnas de Oaxaca* Memorias del Instituto Nacional de Antropología e Historia **2** (Mexico).

CASO, ALFONSO, and IGNACIO BERNAL. 1965. "Ceramics of Oaxaca." *Handbook of Middle American Indians,* R. Wauchope and G. Willey, eds. (8 v. to date, Austin) **3**, 2: pp. 871–895.

CASO, ALFONSO, and D. F. RUBÍN DE LA BORBOLLA. 1936. *Exploraciones en Mitla 1934–1935.* Publ. Instituto Panamericano de Geografía e Historia **21** (Mexico).

CASSÍO, JOSÉ LORENZO. 1940. "La zona arqueológica de 'Cutha' Zapotitlan, Salinas, Puebla, Mexico." *Boletín de la Sociedad Mexicana de Geografía y Estadística* **50**: pp. 115–180.

CHADWICK, ROBERT, and R. S. MACNEISH. 1967. "Codex Borgia and the Venta Salada Phase." *The Prehistory of the Tehuacan Valley,* D. Byers, ed. (2 v. to date, Austin) **1**: pp. 114–131.

Codex Borgia 1903–1909. Elucidated by Eduard Seler (3 v., Berlin).

Codex Fejérvary-Mayer 1901–1902. Elucidated by Eduard Seler (Berlin and London).

Codex Vaticannus No. 3773 (Codex Vaticannus B) 1902-1903. Elucidated by Eduard Seler (Berlin and London).

Códice Chimalpopoca: Anales de Cuauhtitlan y leyendas de los soles 1945. Universidad Nacional Autónoma de México, Instituto de Historia (Mexico).

COE, MICHAEL D. 1961. *La Victoria, an Early Site on the Pacific Coast of Guatemala.* Papers of the Peabody Museum of Archaeology and Ethnology, Harvard University **53** (Cambridge).

Comisión Intersecretarial Coordinadora del Levantamiento de la Carta Geográfica de la Republica México 1958. Map Veracruz 14 Q VI.

COOK, SHERBURNE F. 1939. "Dwelling Construction in the Mixteca." *El México Antiguo* **5**: pp. 375–386.

—— 1949. "Soil Erosion and Population in Central Mexico." *Ibero-Americana* **34**.

COOK, SHERBURNE F., and L. B. SIMPSON. 1948. "The Population of Central Mexico in the Sixteenth Century." *Ibero-Americana* **31**.

COOK DE LEONARD, CARMEN. 1953. "Los Popolocas de Puebla." *Revista Mexicana de Estudios Antropológicos* **8**, 2–3: pp. 423–445.

—— 1961. "The Painted Tribute Record of Tepexi de la Seda." *A.W.C. Townsend en el 25 Aniversario del Instituto Linguistico de Verano* (Mexico), pp. 87–107.

DAHLGREN DE JORDÁN, BARBRO. 1954. *La Mixteca: su cultura e historia prehispanicas* (Mexico).

DELGADO, AGUSTÍN. 1961. *La secuencia arqueológica en el Istmo de Tehuantepec. Los Mayos del sur y sus relaciones con los Nahuas meridionales* (Sociedad Mexicana de Antropología, Octava Mesa Redonda, Mexico).

DRUCKER, PHILIP. 1943. *Ceramic Sequence at Tres Zapotes, Veracruz, Mexico.* Smithsonian Institution, Bureau of American Ethnology, Bulletin **153** (Washington, D. C.).

EKHOLM, GORDON F. 1953. "Notas arqueológicas sobre el Valle de Tuxpan y areas circunvecinas." *Revista Mexicana de Estudios Antropológicos* **8**, 2–3.

EPSTEIN, JEREMIAH F. 1964. "Towards the Systematic Description of Chipped Stone." *Actas y Memorias XXXV Congreso Internacional de Americanistas, México 1962* **1**: pp. 155–169.

ESPEJO, M. A. 1949. "Introducción" (to "Fragmentos de vasijas de barro con decoración en relieve." by C. Seler-Sachs) *El México Antiguo* **7**: pp. 96–104.

FLANNERY, KENT, and A. V. T. KIRKBY, M. J. KIRKBY and A. W. WILLIAMS, JR. 1967. "Farming Systems and Political Growth in Ancient Oaxaca." *Science* **158**, 3800: pp. 445–454.

FOSTER, GEORGE M. 1960. "Archaeological Implications of the Modern Pottery of Acatlan, Puebla, Mexico." *American Antiquity* **26**, 2: pp. 205–214.

FRANCO, JOSÉ LUIS. 1949. "Problemas relativos a la cerámica Azteca." *El México Antiguo* **7**: pp. 162:208.

—— 1955. "Sobre un molde para vasijas con decoración en relieve." *El México Antiguo* **8**: pp. 76–83.

FRIED, MORTON H. 1967. *The Evolution of Political Society* (New York).

GALLEGOS, ROBERTO. 1962. "Exploraciones en Zaachila, Oaxaca." *Boletín del Instituto de Antropología e Historia* **8**: pp. 6–8.

GAMIO, MANUEL. 1922. *La población del valle de Teotihuacan* (Secretaría de Agricultura y Fomento, Dirección de Antropología, Mexico).

GARCÍA PAYÓN, JOSÉ. 1950. "Exploraciones en Xiuhtetelco, Puebla." *Uni-Ver* **2**, 23: pp. 447–476.

GIBSON, CHARLES. 1952. *Tlaxcala in the Sixteenth Century* (New Haven).

GILA, L. H., and F. F. PETERSON and R. B. GROSSMAN. 1965. "The K Horizon: A Master Soil Horizon of Carbonate Accumulation." *Soil Science* **99**, 2: pp. 74–82.

GILA, L. H., and F. F. PETERSON and R. B. GROSSMAN. 1966. "Morphological and Genetic Sequences of Carbonate Accumulation in Desert Soils." *Soil Science* **101**, 5: pp. 347–360.

GORENSTEIN, SHIRLEY. 1963. *The Differential Development of Military and Political Organization in Prehispanic Peru and Mexico* (Ann Arbor).

—— 1966a. "The Differential Development of New World Empires." *Revista Mexicana de Estudios Antropológicos* **20**: pp. 41–67.

—— 1966b. "Choosing a Site to Dig." *Natural History* **75**, 2: 64–67.

—— 1969. "Change in a Protohistoric Community in the Mixteca-Puebla Region of Mexico." Paper read at the 28th annual meeting of the Society for Applied Anthropology, Mexico City.

GRIFFIN, JAMES B., and A. ESPEJO. 1950. "La alfarería correspondiente al ultimo período de occupación Nahua del valle de México." *Tlatelolco a Través de los Tiempos* **11**: pp. 15–66.

HERRERA Y TORDESILLAS, ANTONIO DE. 1947. *Historia general de los hechos de los castellanos en las islas y tierrafirme del mar océano* (Madrid).

Historia Tolteca-Chichimeca 1947. Fuentes para la historia de México. S. Toscano, ed. (Mexico).

ICAZA, FRANCISCO A. DE. 1928. "Miscelánea histórica." *Revista Mexicana de Estudios Historicos* **2**, apendice: pp. 5–112.

JIMÉNEZ MORENO, WIGBERTO. 1942. "El enigma de las olmecas." *Cuadernos Americanos* **5**, 5: pp. 113–145.

—— 1952–1953. "Cronología de la historia de Veracruz." *Revista Mexicana de Estudios Antropológicos* **8**, 2–3: pp. 311–313.

—— 1966. "Mesoamerica Before the Toltecs." *Ancient Oaxaca,* J. Paddock, ed. (Stanford), pp. 1–82.

KINGSBOROUGH, EARL OF. 1831–1848. *Antiquities of Mexico* (9 v., London).

LANDA ABREGO, MARIA ELENA. 1962. *Contribución al estudio de la formación cultural del valle poblana-tlaxcalteca* (Instituto Poblano de Antropología e Historia, Mexico).

LANNING, EDWARD P. 1967. *Peru Before the Incas* (Englewood Cliffs).

LINNÉ, SIGVALD. 1942. *Mexico Highland Cultures. Archaeological Researches at Teotihuacan, Calpulalpan, and Chalchcomulco in 1934/35.* Ethnographical Museum of Sweden, New Series Publication **7** (Stockholm).

LITTMAN, EDWIN. 1957. "Ancient Meosamerican Mortars, Plasters, and Stuccos: Comalco-Part I." *American Antiquity* **23**, 2: pp. 135–140.

MACNEISH, RICHARD S. 1958. "Preliminary Archaeological Investigations in the Sierra de Tamaulipas, Mexico." *Trans. Amer. Philos. Soc.* **48**, 6.

MACNEISH, RICHARD S., A. NELKEN-TERNER and I. WEITLANER DE JOHNSON. 1967. *The Prehistory of the Tehuacan Valley* D. S. Byers, ed. (2 v. to date, Austin) **2**.

MAZIHCATZIN, N. F. 1927. "Descripción de lienzo de Tlaxcala." *Revista Mexicana de Estudios Historicos* **1**, apendice: pp. 59–90.

MEDELLÍN ZENIL, ALFONSO. 1960. *Cerámicas del Totonacapan* (Universidad Veracruzana, Jalapa).

Mesoamerican Notes 1955. Dept. of Anthropology, Mexico City College **4** (Mexico).

MESAROVIĆ, MIHAJLO D. 1968. Systems Theory and Biology (New York).

MIRANDA, F. 1947. "Rasgos de la vegetación de la cuenca del rio de las Balsas." *Revista de la Socieded Mexicana de Historia Natural* **8**: pp. 95–114.

MOSER, CHRISTOPHER. 1969. "Matching Polychrome Sets from Acatlan, Puebla." *American Antiquity* **34**, 4: pp. 480-482.

MUNSELL. 1942. *Munsell Soil Color Charts* (Baltimore).

NAROLL, RAOUL. 1962. "Floor Area and Settlement Population." *American Antiquity* **27**, 4: pp. 587–589.

NICHOLSON, H. B. 1960. "The Mixteca-Puebla Concept in Meosamerican Archaeology." *Men and Cultures* A. Wallace, ed. (Philadelphia): pp. 612–617.

—— 1961. "The Use of the Term 'Mixtec' in Mesoamerican Archaeology." *American Antiquity* **26**, 3, 1: pp. 431–432.

NOGUERA, EDUARDO. 1940. "Excavaciones en Calipan." *El México Antiguo* **5**, 3–5: pp. 63–124.

—— 1945. "Excavaciones en el estado de Puebla." *Anales del Instituto Nacional de Antropología e Historia* **1**: pp. 31–74.

—— 1954. *La cerámica arqueológica de Cholula* (Mexico).

—— 1960. "Relaciones de Oaxaca con Puebla y Tlaxcala: culturas cholulteca, mixteca y zapoteca." *Revista Mexicana de Estudios Antropológicos* **16**: pp. 129–135.

—— 1965. *La cerámica arqueológica de Mesoamerica* (Universidad Nacional Autónoma de México, Instituto de Investigaciones Historicas, Mexico).

O'NEILL, GEORGE C. 1962. *Postclassic Ceramic Stratigraphy at Chalco in the Valley of Mexico* (Ann Arbor).

OBREGON DE LA PARRA, JORGE. 1950. "Tepexi el Viejo, en estado de Puebla." Report in the archives of the Instituto Nacional de Antropología e Historia.

PADDOCK, JOHN. 1953. "Excavations in the Mixteca Alta." *Mesoamerican Notes* **3**.

—— 1960. "Exploraciones en Yagul, Oaxaca." *Revista Mexicana de Estudios Antropológicos* **16**: pp. 91–96.

—— 1966. "Oaxaca in Ancient Mesoamerica." *Ancient Oaxaca* J. Paddock, ed. (Stanford), pp. 83–242.

PAREYÓN MORENO, EDUARDO. 1960. "Exploraciones arqueológicas en Ciudad Vieja de Quiotepec, Oaxaca." *Revista Mexicana de Estudios Antropológicos* **16**: pp. 97–104.

PARSONS, LEE A. 1967. *Bilbao, Guatemala. An Archaeological Study of the Pacific Coast Cotzumalhuapa Region.* Milwaukee Public Museum Publications in Anthropology **11** (Milwaukee).

PASO Y TRONCOSO, FRANCISCO DEL. 1905. "Abecedario de las vistas de los pueblos de la Nueva Spaña." *Papeles de Nueva España* Segunda serie (7 v., Madrid) **1**.

—— 1906. *Papeles de Nueva España,* Segunda Serie (7 v., Madrid) **5**.

PEÑAFIEL, ANTONIO. 1897. *Nomenclatura geográfica de México* (Oficina Tipográfica de la Secretaría de Fomento, Mexico).

POPE, SAXON T. 1962. *Bows and Arrows* (Berkeley and Los Angeles).

RAMON LLEGE, ADELE. 1959. "Utiles de piedra." *Esplendor del México Antiguo,* C. Cook de Leonard, ed. (2 v., Mexico) 2.

RATTRAY, EVELYN. "An Archaeological and Stylistic Study of Coyotlatelco Pottery." *Mesoamerican Notes* **7–8**: pp. 87–211.

ROBERTSON, DONALD. 1966. "The Mixtec Religious Manuscripts." *Ancient Oaxaca,* J. Paddock, ed. (Stanford), pp. 298–312.

ROUSE, IRVING. 1960. "The Classification of Artifacts in Archaeology." *American Antiquity* **25**, 3: pp. 313–323.

—— 1965. "Caribbean Ceramics: A Study in Method and in Theory." *Ceramics and Man,* F. Matson, ed. Viking Fund Publication in Anthropology **41** (New York), pp. 88–103.

SABLOFF, JEREMY A. and R. E. SMITH. 1969. "The Importance of Both Analytic and Taxonomic Classification in the Type-Variety System." *American Antiquity* **34**, 3: pp. 278–285.

SANDERS, WILLIAM T. 1956. "The Central Mexican Symbiotic Region: A Study in Prehistoric Settlement Patterns." *Prehistoric Settlement Patterns in the New World,* Viking Fund Publication in Anthropology **23** (New York), pp. 115–127.

—— 1965. *The Cultural Ecology of the Teotihuacán Valley* (Dept. of Sociology and Anthropology, Pennsylvania State University).

SANDERS, WILLIAM T., and BARBARA PRICE. 1968. *Mesoamerica: The Evolution of a Civilization* (New York).

SELER-SACHS, CECILIE. 1949. "Fragmentos de vasijas de barro con decoración en relieve." *El México Antiguo* **7**: pp. 105–118.

SHEPARD, ANNA O. 1948. *Plumbate: A Mesoamerican Trade Ware.* Carnegie Institution of Washington Publication **573** (Washington, D. C.).

SMILLIE, K. W. 1969. *STATPACKI—An Experiment in the Documentation, Distribution, and Use of a Set of Statistical Programs.* Dept. of Computing Science, University of Alberta Publication **16** (Alberta).

SMITH, ROBERT E., G. WILLEY and J. GIFFORD. 1960. "The Type-Variety Concept as a Basis for the Analysis of Maya Pottery." *American Antiquity* **25**, 3: pp. 330–340.

SPORES, RONALD. 1967. *The Mixtec Kings and Their People* (Norman).

—— 1969. "Settlement, Farming Technology, and Environment in the Nochistlan Valley." *Science* **116**, 3905: pp. 557–568.

TAMAYO, JORGE L. 1946. *Datos para la hidrología de la Republica.* Publicación Instituto Panamericano de Geografía e Historia **84** (Mexico).

—— 1949. *Geografía general de México* (2 v. and atlas, Mexico).

TEZOZOMOC, HERNANDO ALVARADO. 1878. *Crónica Mexicana* (Mexico).

TOLSTOY, PAUL. 1958. "Surface Survey of the Northern Valley of Mexico." *Trans. Amer. Philos. Soc.* **45**, 5.

—— n.d. "Stone, Bone and Antler Tools of Central Mexico from Preclassic to Aztec Times." (Mimeographed.)

TORQUEMADA, FRAY JUAN DE. 1723. *Los veinte i un libros rituales y monarchia indiana* (3 v., Madrid).

VAILLANT, GEORGE C. 1931. "Excavations at Ticoman." *Anthropological Papers of the American Museum of Natural History* **32**, 1.

—— 1944. *The Aztecs of Mexico* (New York).

VIVÓ ESCOTO, JORGE. 1964. "Weather and Climate of Mexico and Central America." *Handbook of Middle American Indians,* R. Wauchope and R. West, eds. (8 v. to date, Austin) **1**: pp. 187–215.

VIVÓ ESCOTO, JORGE, and J. GÓMEZ. 1946. *Climotología de México.* Publicación Instituto Panamericano de Geografía e Historia **19** (Mexico).

WAGNER, PHILIP. 1964. "Natural Vegetation of Middle America." *Handbook of Middle American Indians,* R. Wauchope and G. Willey, eds. (8 v. to date, Austin) **1**: pp. 216–264.

WALKER, T. B. 1967. "Formation of Red Beds in Modern and Ancient Deserts." *Geological Society of America Bulletin* **78**, 3: pp. 353–368.

WALLRATH, MATTHEW. 1967. "Excavations in the Tehuantepec Region, Mexico." *Trans. Amer. Philos. Soc.* **57**, 2.

WEST, ROBERT. 1964. "Surface Configuration and Associated Geology of Middle America." *Handbook of Middle American Indians,* R. Wauchope and G. Willey, eds. (8 v. to date, Austin) **1**: pp. 33–83.

WICKE, CHARLES. 1966. "Tomb 30 at Yagul and the Zaachila Tombs." *Ancient Oaxaca,* J. Paddock, ed. (Stanford), pp. 336–344.

YADIN, YIGAEL. 1963. *The Art of Warfare in Biblical Lands in the Light of Archaeological Study* (2 v., New York).

ZAVALA, SILVIO. 1938. *Francisco del Paso y Troncoso. Su misión en Europa 1892–1916* (Mexico).